Cambridge

Elements in Psychology ...
edited by
Kenneth D. Keith
University of San Diego

CONCEPT AND METHOD IN CROSS-CULTURAL AND CULTURAL PSYCHOLOGY

Ype H. Poortinga
Tilburg University

CAMBRIDGE
UNIVERSITY PRESS

CAMBRIDGE
UNIVERSITY PRESS

University Printing House, Cambridge CB2 8BS, United Kingdom

One Liberty Plaza, 20th Floor, New York, NY 10006, USA

477 Williamstown Road, Port Melbourne, VIC 3207, Australia

314–321, 3rd Floor, Plot 3, Splendor Forum, Jasola District Centre, New Delhi – 110025, India

103 Penang Road, #05–06/07, Visioncrest Commercial, Singapore 238467

Cambridge University Press is part of the University of Cambridge.

It furthers the University's mission by disseminating knowledge in the pursuit of education, learning, and research at the highest international levels of excellence.

www.cambridge.org
Information on this title: www.cambridge.org/9781108827614
DOI: 10.1017/9781108908320

First published 2021

A catalogue record for this publication is available from the British Library.

ISBN 978-1-108-82761-4 Paperback
ISSN 2515-3986 (online)
ISSN 2515-3943 (print)

Concept and Method in Cross-Cultural and Cultural Psychology

Elements in Psychology and Culture

DOI: 10.1017/9781108908320
First published online: October 2021

Ype H. Poortinga
Tilburg University

Author for correspondence: Ype H. Poortinga, Y.H.Poortinga@uvt.nl

Abstract: An overview is given of cross-cultural psychology and cultural psychology, focusing on theory and methodology. In Section 1, historical developments in research are traced; findings indicate that initially extensive psychological differences tend to shrink when more carefully designed studies are conducted. Section 2 addresses the conceptualization of "culture" and of "a culture." For psychological research, the notion of "culture" is considered too vague; more focal explanatory concepts are required. Section 3 describes methodological issues, taking the idea of the empirical cycle as a lead for both qualitative and quantitative research. Pitfalls in research design and data analysis of behavior-comparative studies and the need for replication are discussed. Section 4 suggests moving beyond research on causal relationships and incorporating additional questions, addressing the function and the development of behavior patterns in ontogenetic, phylogenetic, and historical time. Section 5 emphasizes the need for applied research serving the global village.

Keywords: conceptualization of "culture," cross-cultural psychology, cultural psychology, design and data analysis, Tinbergen's questions

ISBNs: 9781108827614 (PB), 9781108908320 (OC)
ISSNs: 2515-3986 (online), 2515-3943 (print)

Contents

Introduction

Every time I hear the word culture I release the safety on my 9 mm.

Banksy

It is evident that between human populations, especially between societies, there are differences in overt behavior repertoires and in (covert) understandings. Striking examples include traffic rules, spoken and written language, dress codes, and religious practices. The most common term to capture such differences is "culture." Any population tends to be attributed its own culture, and behavior differences between populations are referred to as "cultural" or "cross-cultural" differences. These are the subject of study in cultural anthropology; language and communication sciences; ethology; and various subfields of psychology, such as cross-cultural psychology, psychology and culture, cultural psychology, and indigenous psychology. The term to be used in this Element for these subfields of psychology is "cross-cultural and cultural psychology," abbreviated (c)cp.

"Culture" has multiple meanings, including, but not limited to, the following: (i) antecedent conditions for human behavior (e.g., climate, GDP, modes of subsistence), (ii) context in which individual behavior takes place (e.g., society), (iii) attribution of meaning to actions and events, and (iv) the outcome of events or processes that took place in the past (e.g., evolution of culture). In (c)cp, "culture" is often attributed causal or agentic qualities. The introduction of the series on culture and psychology in which this Element is published mentions "the pervasive influence of culture on individual human behavior." Other examples include the following:

"Culture plays a powerful causal role in determining human behavior" (Mesoudi, Whiten, & Laland, 2006, p. 331)

"[T]he myriad ways in which culture shapes emotional life" (Tsai & Clobert, 2019, p. 292)

"Culture shapes electrocortical responses during emotion suppression" (Murata, Moser, & Kitayama, 2013, p. 595)

"[C]ulture influences the prevalence of different types of self-concept" (Kashima & Gelfand, 2012, p. 509)

"The relation of children's emotion knowledge to internalizing problems was moderated by culture" (Doan & Wang, 2018, p. 689)

An important connotation of "culture" is that observed behavior differences are an expression of broader differences in underlying psychological traits and processes. Supposedly, people *do* different things because in some way they *are* different psychologically. In this Element, "culture" and its connotations are examined with a focus on conceptualization and research methodology.

Throughout the Element, it is accepted as axiomatic that social and ecological context is important for the explanation and understanding of human behavior. (C)cp is of interest scientifically because planned selection of populations and contexts allows the identification of factors that affect behavior variation and the terms in which variation can be explained. A wealth of studies report differences; the extant literature is far less explicit about how much patterns of psychological functioning are similar across all of humanity. This emphasis on differences is seen as a danger; it easily leads to stereotyping "others." The main point to be made here is that sound theory and methodology are essential prerequisites for dependable knowledge.

Equally axiomatic is the conviction that (c)cp has applied relevance. In a world that rapidly acquires the characteristics of a global village, it is an unmistakable contribution of research in (c)cp that attention is drawn to differences in human behavior. There is a need to make sense of both behavior diversity and communality. Even though applications are not the main theme of this Element, applicability is the ultimate justification for the pursuit of scientific knowledge. At the basis of large differences in behavior repertoires between humans living in various contexts are conditions of poverty and inequality, as opposed to affluence and security. These should be of concern to researchers in (c)cp.

1 Historical Overview

This section briefly reviews a selection of research traditions since the 1960s when (c)cp began to emerge as a distinguishable subfield within psychology, and perception and cognition were major areas of research. Beginning in the 1980s, social psychological research became a dominant theme, with value dimensions as a major focus. Also mentioned in this section is research on emotions, psycholinguistics, and cultural neuroscience. Throughout, a pervasive historical trend is noted: with a new topic or approach, initial claims about big and important population differences in psychological functioning tend to be reported that do not hold up in later more carefully designed and critical empirical studies.

1.1 Perception

Rivers (1901) conducted an early psychological study in the Torres Strait Islands. He was impressed with the sensory acuity and great attention to detail of the local inhabitants, but he believed that the development of such a high level of perceptual skills was an impediment to cognitive development: "The predominant attention of the [local person] to concrete things around him may act as an obstacle to higher mental development" (p. 45). The idea of a trade-off in ontogenetic development between various psychological dispositions later became known as a "compensation hypothesis" (Deręgowski, 1980). In the mid-twentieth century, there were less-encompassing versions of this hypothesis, suggesting a trade-off in the development of various perceptual modalities, notably vision and hearing. Persons of European descent would be more oriented toward visual stimuli, while Africans would excel in auditory tasks. In support of this viewpoint, various arguments were mentioned, such as the apparent ease with which unschooled Africans could learn Western languages like English and French and their strong sense of rhythm and music. However, quasi-experimental studies failed to show empirical support (Deręgowski, 1989), and today compensation hypotheses are only of historical interest.

Consistent findings of differences do exist, notably for susceptibility to simple visual illusions, such as the Müller-Lyer illusion and the horizontal-vertical illusion. Differences in susceptibility scores can be linked to observable antecedent factors in the natural environment. Segall et al. (1966) conducted a landmark study across several environments. One of the postulated antecedents of susceptibility for these illusions was the degree of "carpenteredness"; in societies where carpenters and other artisans have shaped the physical environment, one finds many more orthogonal angles in buildings and street corners than in traditional societies. Another factor was the degree to which the environment is open (wide vistas) or closed in (forest or buildings). Segall et al. (1966) found systematic relationships of these environmental antecedents with susceptibility for such illusions as mentioned. Later studies have supported these findings (for reviews, see Deręgowski, 1989; www.illusionsindex.org).

We should note three points that in various ways will come up again later in this Element. First, illusion effects as mentioned are apparently present in all human populations. Second, context matters; even for such a simple figure as the horizontal-vertical illusion, consisting of only two line segments, differences in the natural environment affect the strength of the illusion effect. Third, sweeping generalizations, as suggested by various compensation hypotheses, did not pass critical analysis.

1.2 Cognition

Items of knowledge and cognitive skills (e.g., doing arithmetic) are inherently situational and highly contextualized, and large variations across populations are evident. However, it is less clear what this implies for cross-cultural invariance or variations in underlying cognitive processes and functions (e.g., deductive reasoning). Three classical topics are mentioned briefly: research on syllogisms, Piagetian research, and research based on the postulate of an East-West contrast in social-cognitive orientation.

Research on syllogisms became prominent in (c)cp through studies reported by Luria (1971). He found strikingly poor performances of illiterate respondents from Central Asia when they were asked to solve syllogistic problems referring to situations beyond their own experience. In sharp contrast, respondents with only a few years of formal education deduced logically correct answers. Luria interpreted these findings as support for Vygotsky's (1978) idea that higher mental functions, such as abstract thinking, are "culturally mediated"; they originate at the level of a society (i.e., a population with frequent interactions between individual members) before they can become individual functions. Scribner (1979) provided a less sweeping account. In a study in Liberia with think-aloud protocols, she found that unschooled participants did follow principles of logic to solve syllogisms, but the basis of their reasoning was their own prior experience rather than the premises mentioned by an experimenter. In other words, Scribner's respondents did not start from the premises presented to them, but more from what they knew to be factually true, and starting from there they applied common logic. This study is one example of Cole and colleagues' tradition of "contextualized cognition." In an early publication, they concluded that "cultural differences in cognition reside more in the situations to which particular cognitive processes are applied, than in the existence of a process in one cultural group and its absence in another" (Cole et al., 1971, p. 233).

Major differences in abstract thinking as reported by Luria have been attributed widely to differences in ways of thinking between literate and illiterate peoples (see Segall et al., 1990, chap. 5, for an overview). An important challenge to such contrasts came from a study by Scribner and Cole (1981), who demonstrated that literacy is not a kind of watershed for cognitive functioning. They found that for groups with different scripts and traditions of schooling in Liberia, performance on various cognitive tasks was attuned to the particularities of their experiences and the curricula in their education. It may be noted that Cole (e.g., Cole, 1996) does endorse the idea of mediation of cognitive processes, but at the level of specific skills and cognitions, rather than at the level of cognitive functions that become manifest in broad domains of behavior.

Another tradition in cognition research, clearly illustrating changes over time from broader to more specific interpretations of differences, is Piagetian research. Piaget (e.g., Piaget, 1970) postulated a well-known hierarchical sequence of three stages in cognitive development: sensorimotor, concrete-operational, and formal thinking. In a review of early cross-cultural studies, Dasen (1972) reported that compared with Western populations, populations with low formal education showed major delays in the age of onset of the concrete-operational stage. Sometimes this stage was not even reached at all by a substantial proportion of participants. This finding essentially was overturned in research showing that twelve-year-old children who would not spontaneously use concrete-operational reasoning often would do so after a brief learning episode. Dasen (1984) argued that a distinction should be made between performance and competence; obviously, the competence for concrete-operational reasoning had to be available to a child if the performance of such reasoning could be solicited with little effort.

An influential tradition was started when Nisbett and colleagues postulated a broad distinction between East Asia and the West in holistic or dialectical versus analytic thinking (Nisbett et al., 2001; Peng & Nisbett, 1999). This difference is seen as rooted in social orientation, with East Asians reflecting a more interdependent construal of the self and Europeans (including European Americans) a more independent construal of the self (Markus & Kitayama, 1991). The East-West dichotomy has been the basis for numerous empirical studies on a wide range of cognitive and social psychological variables seen as correlates of this broad distinction. Typically, they have reported supportive findings (for overviews, see Cohen & Kitayama, 2019; Kitayama & Cohen, 2007).

There are reasons to question the validity of a broad dimension of East-West differences as proposed. Probably the most critical point is that the typical two-sample studies of this tradition, with relatively small samples seeking convergent evidence, are vulnerable to false positive outcomes; in fact, they have started to show poor replicability (see Section 3.4). Another reason is a tendency of authors to ignore or reinterpret results that an outsider would see as negative outcomes for the underlying theory. For example, Wong et al. (2018) found that Canadians of European descent showed better memory for backgrounds than Chinese participants did, a result not in line with expectations (Masuda & Nisbett, 2001). The authors construed an additional argument to tune their finding to the theory but appear not to have considered that the finding actually might be in conflict with the theory. A third reason is that negative findings tend to be ignored. Studies by Rayner and colleagues (Evans et al., 2009; Rayner et al., 2007) failed to show expected differences in eye movement patterns and recognition memory, suggesting that both Americans and Chinese use the same rather than different strategies in scene perception and memory. In the authoritative *Handbook of Cultural Psychology* (Cohen & Kitayama, 2019), this work is mentioned in passing as relevant, but implications are not considered.

A fourth reason to question this major East-West dimension derives from studies with multiple measures of both cognitive and social variables (Na et al.,

2010; Na et al., 2020). Correlations between the measures within samples were negligible, not only across the two domains but also between measures within the cognitive domain and within the social domain. The authors argue that the measures pertain to constructs consisting of loosely related attributes that need not lead to consistent individual differences. At the very least, this argument implies a major deviation from earlier theorizing that clearly presumed psychological coherence across the two domains and definitely within each domain. By common psychometric standards, the findings of Na and colleagues should have been deemed incompatible with the broad theory that they examined.

1.3 Psycholinguistics

An obvious starting point is Whorf's (1956) hypothesis, also known as the Sapir-Whorf hypothesis or the linguistic relativity hypothesis. This hypothesis postulates that through its words and grammar, a language shapes the thinking and ideas of the speakers of that language. The principle that language is a vehicle for thinking is widely endorsed, but there is debate about the extent to which differences between languages can be associated with differences in perception and thinking. Two topics have become real battlegrounds: color categories and frames of reference used in spatial orientation.

Whorf's conjecture implies that color names in a language will divide a map of all visible colors (the color space) in a language-specific fashion. Support for this idea came from ethnographic research reporting color terms in various languages for which there is no corresponding term in English (and vice versa) (e.g., Ray, 1952). Berlin and Kay (1969) followed a more systematic approach. They asked speakers of several languages to name basic color terms (like red, green, blue, etc., for English) in their mother tongue and to indicate for each of these terms the best matching color in the Munsell color system (www.munsell .com). Across languages, the selected colors turned out to cluster and these clusters occupied only a small part of the total space of visible colors. Berlin and Kay (1969, p. 10) concluded that "color categorization is not random and the foci of basic color terms are similar in all languages." However, this was not the end of the controversy. Roberson et al. (2004, 2000) conducted field studies among populations with a limited number of basic color terms (Berinmo in Papua New Guinea and Himba in Namibia). They showed that on some tasks, respondents perform better with distinctions from their own language than with the color categories derived by Berlin and Kay. More extensive evidence comes from the World Color Survey (Kay et al., 2009), covering the color lexicons of 110 non-written languages in terms of the Munsell system. Analysis of these data has indicated more variation between individual speakers of a language than between languages as well as a clustering according to linguistic families. However, overall variation is limited (Bimler, 2007; Lindsey & Brown, 2009). Thus, there appear to be strong regularities in color categorization that to an important extent invalidate Whorf's far-reaching claims.

Research on spatial orientation hinges on a distinction between an ego-referenced, or relative, orientation and an absolute orientation. An example may help make this distinction clear. Suppose an observer is facing a table and a chair. Using the ego-referenced orientation, this observer may say that the chair is on the left side of the table. After moving to the other side of the table, the same observer will then say that the chair is on the right side of the table. A speaker with an absolute orientation will use the same phrase in both instances, as the position of the chair in relation to the table has not changed. This speaker could say, for example, that the chair is to the east of the table. The rising or setting sun, or some other conspicuous feature in the natural environment of a community, such as a mountain, can serve as a standard for absolute orientation (e.g., the chair could be said to be on the side of the table away from the East or away from the mountain). Levinson and colleagues (e.g., Levinson, 2003; Majid et al., 2004) found common use of an absolute orientation in speakers of more than fifteen languages. Using a formulation in line with the original Whorfian hypothesis, Majid et al. (2004, p. 113) referred to "profound linguistic effects on cognition."

A turning point has been a series of studies by Dasen and Mishra (2010) based on a variety of data in various populations. These studies provided a differentiated view with more nuance. They did show evidence of extensive use of an absolute orientation on Bali, in India, and in Nepal but also found that the use of an absolute or relative frame of reference could be task-dependent. Moreover, when asked for an explanation, participants could make use of ego-referenced language to explain answers based on an absolute frame of reference, and vice versa. An example is an ego-referenced alignment of objects by a study participant that is explained subsequently in terms referring to the absolute orientation. Dasen and Mishra (2010) concluded that individuals possess the basic processes needed for both an absolute and an ego-oriented frame of reference, deflating the original claims.

1.4 Emotions

During much of the twentieth century, it was widely accepted that the repertoire of emotions was acquired in the process of socialization, at least to a considerable extent (e.g., Birdwhistell, 1970). New evidence came from studies based on a theory postulating that a small set of six or seven basic emotions is found universally, each of which is expressed through a typical muscular contraction pattern in the face. Ekman and Friesen (1971) reported that respondents in Papua New Guinea, unfamiliar with European faces, recognized these basic emotions in posed photographs of European Americans. In addition, raters in the United States of America often correctly identified photographs of such expressions produced by participants in Papua New Guinea.

Further arguments for population specificity of emotions came from the observation that there are words present in other languages for which there is no matching word in English (Lutz, 1988; Russell, 1991, 1994). This culture-specific or relativist position (see Section 3.1) was taken up in the school of cultural psychology. Setting a clear agenda for identifying essential differences in emotional functioning, Kitayama and Markus (1994, p. 1) wrote: "Specifically, we wish to establish that emotion can be fruitfully conceptualized as being social in nature, or in Lutz's (1988) words, as being 'anything but natural.'" In other words, emotions are learned and the emotional repertoire that a person develops is dependent on the social context.

Strong versions of both the universalist and the relativist perspectives turned out to be vulnerable. On the one hand, face recognition from posed photographs was far from perfect; there was a considerable proportion of unexplained variance in facial recognition studies (Russell, 1994). On the other hand, reliance on verbal labeling of emotional experiences was also questionable, because the absence or presence of an emotion word need not have much influence on patterns of reactions to emotion-soliciting situations. For example, the Rarámuri, an indigenous group of subsistence farmers in Northern Mexico, do not have a word for "shame" as distinct from "guilt." Breugelmans and Poortinga (2006) asked Rarámuri participants to rate a set of situations on a broad set of emotion characteristics that previously had been found to differentiate shame from guilt in an international student sample. For most of these characteristics, a pattern of differentiation was found for the Rarámuri participants similar to that of the students and also to that of Javanese famers, known to have separate terms for "guilt" and "shame" in their language.

Further research on facial expressions has continued to show evidence of wide recognition of basic emotions, also beyond staged photographs. For example, Matsumoto and Willingham (2006) analyzed facial expressions of individual winners and losers from thirty-five countries in Olympic matches and concluded that spontaneous facial expressions of athletes from all over the world point to common emotions. A more recent review (Barrett et al., 2019) challenges a wide range of sources of evidence in facial recognition studies traditionally interpreted as pointing to common emotions. Barrett et al. (2019)

demand high reliability and configuration specificity across a broad range of populations, including populations in remote areas, to justify the conclusion that a distinctive configuration for an emotion category exists. They argue that the meaning of facial movements is too variable and context-dependent to justify such a conclusion.

It may well be that the standards required by Barrett et al. (2019) are too strict, but with unclear criteria for universality, it is difficult to resolve current debates. Perhaps the best representation for now is the notion of a common emotion language with local dialects that explain both communality and an in-group advantage in emotion recognition (Elfenbein, 2013; Elfenbein & Ambady, 2002). This is in line with results from other research, using ratings of emotion situations, that shows invariance of the factorial structure of emotion components (e.g., Fontaine, Veirman, & Groenvynck, 2013). It is also in line with everyday observations to the effect that, on the one hand, errors of communication between individuals appear to be more frequent across than within populations and that, on the other hand, poetry and TV serials, which heavily depend on communication of emotions, can travel across languages, countries, and regions (Berry et al., 2011).

1.5 Values

Much research in (c)cp has a social psychological perspective. Of the broad range of research traditions, only values, the most dominant topic during the past four decades, is discussed here. Attention for values exploded after Hofstede (1980) postulated four dimensions distinguishing populations at country level, that is, individualism, power distance, masculinity, and uncertainty avoidance. Triandis (1989, 1996) further elaborated the dimension of individualism as individualism-collectivism, building on an earlier distinction in sociology between *Gesellschaft* (society) and *Gemeinschaft* (community). The individualism-collectivism dimension has been linked to the dichotomy of independent construal of the self and interdependent construal of the self, formulated by Markus and Kitayama (1991), and to the broad East-West dichotomy presented earlier. Although Hofstede added some dimensions later, the original four continue to be used widely, for example, in marketing research (e.g., Song et al., 2018). In the *Journal of Cross-Cultural Psychology*, studies conducted as recently as 2019 use individualism-collectivism as an unquestioned antecedent for some differences between samples from an East Asian country and the United States or Canada, even when results do not appear to fit expectations (e.g., Bebko et al., 2019). In the meantime, a variety of conceptual, methodological, psychometric, and empirical concerns have been raised.

Various authors have mentioned that individualism-collectivism is too broad a dimension for critical examination (Jahoda, 2011; Segall, 1996). Consequently, the dimension is beyond analysis of validity (or falsifiability). An unanswered conceptual question is what high ratings on a value item actually represent. A high score for a value item usually is taken to mean that the respondent sees that value as important or desirable in an absolute sense. However, the notion of "diminishing marginal utility" (Maseland & Van Hoorn, 2009) suggests that we rate as important what we perceive as lacking in our lives.

Spector et al. (2001) examined the psychometric properties of Hofstede's Values Survey Module (1994 edition) in a large replication study. They found inadequate internal consistencies, at both the individual level and the country level and failed to replicate the expected factorial structure at the country level. Apparently, the classification of individual respondents as individualists or collectivists was subject to a large margin of error. Also, there have been frequent failures to obtain country differences that were expected; telling is the lack of support in numerous studies for the idea that Japanese people should be more collectivist than US Americans (e.g., Matsumoto, 1999; Takano & Sogon, 2008). In a large meta-analysis, Oyserman et al. (2002, p. 3) notoriously found "European Americans were not more individualistic than African Americans, or Latinos, and not less collectivistic than Japanese or Koreans." Schimmack et al. (2005) reported very low correlations between the country scores obtained by Oyserman et al. (2002) and individualism-collectivism measurements in the Hofstede tradition. Schimmack et al. (2005) saw this as due to response styles and called for correction. However, even if such a correction would harmonize findings, serious questions remain about findings from previous studies with uncorrected data and the validity of the underlying theorizing of either Hofstede or Oyserman and colleagues, or perhaps both.

To conclude this brief overview, two comments may be added. First, although the validity of individualism-collectivism as a major value dimension is in serious doubt, this discussion is not meant to play down findings of differences between countries on scales, like those of Hofstede (1980) or Schwartz (1992, 2012). Factor analysis of international survey data in these traditions shows, before factor rotation, a large first factor that reflects a manifold of variables centering on affluence (see Section 5.1). Second, although the concept of values remains strong in (c)cp (Fischer, 2018), there has been a shift to less-encompassing distinctions. One example is the concept of "social axioms" (Leung & Bond, 2004) that taps into beliefs people have about the world. Another example is a general shift from values to norms that are more easily linked to external conditions and domains of situations (Gelfand et al., 2011).

1.6 Cultural Neuroscience

A fairly recent field of research in (c)cp is cultural neuroscience, which involves two major streams of research, one emphasizing psychophysiological measurements, the other genetic variation. In both streams, individualism-collectivism and the related East-West dichotomy have been a dominant frame for explaining differences. Psychophysiological studies in (c)cp have made use of various methods, including EEG and evoked response potentials (ERPs) to record reactions to stimuli, but most salient is functional magnetic resonance imaging (fMRI), a method to measure small changes in blood flow to various parts of the brain. In fMRI studies, the brain is divided into a large number of volumetric units, called voxels, for the purpose of data analysis. Results are typically presented in pictures highlighting areas of the brain that are more active during a task or, in (c)cp studies, showing statistically significant differences in activity between a European American sample and an Asian (or Asian American) sample (e.g., Chiao et al., 2009; Hedden et al., 2008).

Vul et al. (2009) demonstrated that fMRI studies are highly vulnerable to false-positive outcomes. With a large number of voxels and small samples of participants (typically $n \leq 15$ and even as low as $n = 10$), statistically significant findings are bound to occur. In addition, the region of the brain examined, the region of interest (ROI), tends to be large and even post hoc findings tend to be interpreted as evidence for postulated population differences (see Chiao et al., 2009, for an extreme instance of this tendency). This raises serious doubts about the findings of any single study. From the literature, one may gain the impression that across studies there has been an accumulation of evidence with significant differences between East Asian and European American samples reported repeatedly (e.g., Han & Northoff, 2008). However, the rates of false positives can be staggering, especially if the ROIs are large and/or vaguely defined. The weakness of analysis and interpretation is demonstrated dramatically in a recent project in which the same fMRI data were analyzed by a large number of laboratories; choices of settings for parameters (the "analysis pipeline") led to important differences in outcomes (Botvinik-Nezer et al., 2020). In my view, the potential significance for (c)cp of psychophysiological variables can hardly be overestimated. In principle, such variables can be less sensitive to issues of bias and lack of equivalence than psychometric scales (see Section 3.3.2). However, with piecemeal small studies this potential has not been and cannot be realized.

Cultural genomics, the other branch of cultural neuroscience, analyzes behavior correlates of differences in the distributions of genetic variations between human populations (called polymorphisms or alleles) and the interactions of such variations with ecological and social contexts. The scope of this area of research can be gained from review articles (e.g., Chen & Moyzis, 2018). Perhaps even more than studies with physiological measures, research on genetic variations across populations can be qualified as an exciting development for (c)cp. The required size of samples, especially for exploratory studies covering the entire genome (GWAS studies; e.g., Lee et al., 2018) is an impediment. Early studies appear to be open to similar criticisms as fMRI research (Poortinga, 2015), but it may be too early for a broad evaluation.

1.7 Conclusion

For various traditions across major areas of (c)cp, this section has illustrated how initially sweeping claims of differences between populations tend to shrink over time. Evidence of such trends is mostly indirect, as it is derived from studies that tend to differ in methods and populations. Direct evidence can be derived from studies estimating proportions of variance for populations and for individuals nested in populations. With questionnaire studies of values and personality traits, country differences have turned out to be much smaller than individual differences. For example, in an analysis of a large body of data collected with the Schwartz Values Scale, Fischer and Schwartz (2011, p. 1132) found that "on average, country differences accounted for only 11% or 12% of the variance in self-ratings." McCrae and Terraciano (2008) analyzed ratings of others (i.e., someone well known to a respondent) by college students in fifty countries on the Big Five dimensions of the Five Factor Model (FFM) of personality. In this data set only 4.0 percent of the total variance could be attributed to country. Evidently, estimates as mentioned are much lower than both laypeople and researchers tend to expect (Fischer, 2020).

Brouwers et al. (2004) showed explicitly that too much emphasis is often placed on differences. These authors analyzed hypotheses postulated in empirical studies published in the *Journal of Cross-Cultural Psychology*. For each hypothesis, they noted whether or not a difference between populations was predicted, and whether the prediction was supported. The results showed the following: "Of all hypotheses testing articles (N = 89), 62.9% expected to find only differences, whereas 25.8% found only differences. In contrast, 28.1% expected to find a combination of differences and similarities, whereas as many as 70.8% found such a combination" (p. 258). The large discrepancies between expectations and outcomes suggest that researchers in (c)cp are strongly biased toward expecting differences between human populations rather than invariance. This raises an ugly question: could the field of (c)cp perhaps be overemphasizing differences and contributing to stereotyping "others" as being different from "us"?

2 Conceptualization

The key concept in (c)cp to deal with differences between human populations in overt and covert behavior is "culture." In this section, thematic differences between schools of (c)cp are mentioned, especially the bewildering array of definitions of "culture." The question is asked whether for research in (c)cp the use of this concept should not be abandoned. Questions are also raised about the notion of "a culture" that traditionally referred to a population defined by common descent and living in a circumscribed geographical location but presently tends to be used also for ad hoc groupings. A further point of discussion involves the various ways in which data are interpreted, ranging from broad and inclusive to narrow and more precise inferences.

2.1 Conceptualizations of "Culture"

The academic discipline for which differences in behavior between populations are the focus of study is cultural anthropology (e.g., Tylor, 1871/1958). A widely shared objective among cultural anthropologists is "to build a truly comparative science of human variation" (Kuper & Marks, 2011, p. 166). (C)cp as a field of study has embraced this ideal. By doing so, it also inherited a nagging problem, namely how to define the object of study: "culture." There is enormous variety in its definitions. In an often quoted analysis, Kroeber and Kluckhohn (1952) presented many of these and added their own lengthy definition. That definition amounts to a listing of what cultural anthropologists of various traditions had studied, including, "patterns," "systems," and "ideas." In (c)cp, Soudijn et al. (1990) rated 128 definitions on 34 categories. A factor analysis resulted in five factors showing only limited correlations with the major distinctions made by Kroeber and Kluckhohn. Soudijn et al. advocated an eclectic approach in which researchers have considerable freedom to choose their own position. Baldwin et al. (2006, p. 24) went a step further and argued that "culture" is to be seen as "an empty sign that people fill with meaning from their own academic backgrounds or personal experiences."

An uncomfortable consequence is that when the term "culture" is used, one cannot know what it refers to. A need for a concept of "culture" is widely acknowledged, also in (c)cp (Jahoda, 2012). Richerson and Boyd (2005, p. 18) formulate it succinctly: "Culture exists." However, if a concept cannot be defined, it acquires the same status as a deity in a religion; even though its existence cannot be captured by any measurement method, for the believer the interventions of the deity are evident. To reflect its questionable conceptual status, in this Element the term "culture" has been placed between quotation marks.

In the approaches to "culture" found in (c)cp, some major categories can be distinguished. One distinction is between "culture" as internal or as external to the person (Berry et al., 2011, chap. 1). Climate, affluence, mode of subsistence (how people make a living), and political organization of the society are aspects of the external context that affect a person's behavior repertoire. Much of the language, religion, beliefs, and habits in a person's social environment are internalized during ontogenetic development and can be qualified as internal context. A second distinction – much discussed toward the end of the twentieth century – is between universalist and relativist approaches. In universalism, the focus is on how different ecological and social environments affect common human psychological functions and processes, and how they lead to, enable, or facilitate differences in behavior repertoires. In relativism, the focus is on how psychological functions and processes themselves are the outcome of inter-actions between organism and context. Discussions in Section 1, for example on emotions, reflect the two positions.

These two dichotomies can serve to identify three, sometimes overlapping, research traditions or schools in (c)cp: cross-cultural psychology, indigenous psychologies, and cultural psychology. All three have long historical roots (e.g., Jahoda, 1992; Jahoda & Krewer, 1997) but are relatively young as fields of research with dedicated handbooks, journals, and conferences. The oldest of the three, cross-cultural psychology, started to emerge in the 1960s. This school had, and continues to have, a comparative perspective and emphasizes eco-logical as well as social context (Berry et al., 2011). Being of North American and European origin, Western psychological theories and methods were the starting point and were applied elsewhere. Researchers in this tradition presume "psychic unity" of humankind, that is, psychological functions and processes should be found universally, although their behavioral manifestations may differ considerably. Overall, this school follows twentieth-century thinking in psychology and its methodology (tests and scales and experiments), treating "culture," or some aspect of it, as a variable or as a quasi-experimental condi-tion. An Achilles' heel is that across populations, psychological measurement methods are likely to unequally represent the targeted psychological traits and processes, resulting in "bias" or "lack of equivalence." This has serious impli-cations for the comparison of data (see Section 3).

With the expansion of psychology as an academic discipline, psychologists in non-Western countries increasingly realized that bias in Western psychology was not limited to items (item bias) or even entire instruments (method bias).

Theoretical formulations and the associated operationalizations in instruments also tend to be context bound; most psychological concepts have their origin in Western countries and world views. A further and even more serious level of bias was recognized, namely that psychological research, also in (c)cp, predominantly addresses concerns of people in Western societies but is hardly directed at major issues of people in the majority world, such issues as poverty and illiteracy (Poortinga, 1999; see Section 5). The need to have a psychology for and from local people led to various attempts at building an indigenous psychology, for example, in Africa (Mkhize, 2004), India (Sinha, 1997), and Mexico (Diaz-Guerrero, 1975).

The need for indigenization in the sense of making psychology locally relevant has hardly been a matter of dispute. It was increasingly evident even to Western researchers that psychology as a Western enterprise should be qualified as the indigenous psychology of only a section of the world's population (Berry et al., 2011). Two approaches emerged. Some authors see indigenization as an intermediate stage toward the development of a common and universally shared psychology, transcending Western preoccupations and enriching psychology with other insights (Adair & Diaz-Loving, 1999; Pondicherry Manifesto of Indian Psychology, 2002). Others insist on the need for essentially different psychologies, taking a relativist perspective (Kim, Yang, & Hwang, 2006). From the latter perspective the use of common methods and instruments across populations can only lead to false results.

A relativist orientation was also at the basis of the third school, cultural psychology, that has become the dominant school of (c)cp in North America. Although emerging somewhat later, it was developed separately from the two other schools. To an important extent, its base was in cultural anthropology, in movements that conceive of "culture" as the medium in which human life evolves or as located in the minds of people, emphasizing meaning rather than overt behavior and external context (Geertz, 1973). In a foundational paper, Shweder (1990, p. 3) defined cultural psychology as "the study of intentional worlds. It is the study of personal functioning in particular intentional worlds." He replaced the notion of psychic unity with the motto that "culture and psyche make each other up." At about the same time, Markus and Kitayama (1991) endorsed the idea that psychological processes are "not just influenced by culture, but are thoroughly culturally constituted" (p. 66). Such a relativist orientation continues to underlie conceptualization in cultural psychology.

However, most researchers in the school of cultural psychology do not adopt a relativist methodology. Studies of East-West differences in cognition and in cultural neuroscience, discussed in Section 1, usually follow quasi-experimental designs and traditional Western measurement methods with no local adaptation of stimuli and items (beyond translation). In fact, the rejection of psychological universalism hardly appears to imply limitations on the comparison of psychological data. Notions of bias and lack of equivalence of scores (see Section 3) are largely absent, even in major handbooks (see Cohen & Kitayama, 2019; Kitayama & Cohen, 2007). In this school, psychological functioning is held to be influenced thoroughly, or even defined, by "culture." However, one gains the impression that psychological measurements and assessment instruments somehow escape the cultural specificity that affects behavior in all other aspects (for an exception, see Heine et al., 2002). Obviously, bias in methods leads to bias in conclusions and misrepresentation, casting doubt on reported findings (see Section 3.3.2).

With the expansion of cultural psychology also came new theoretical approaches. Hong et al. (2000) focused on individuals who are living or have been living in more than one society (i.e., "people who have internalized two cultures to the extent that both cultures are alive inside of them," p. 710). They called their approach "dynamic constructivism," proposing that such persons can switch between "cultural lenses," a process called "cultural frame switching"; items of cultural knowledge become operative in specific situations. Such switching can be studied through priming of research participants with symbols from different societal contexts (e.g., icons like a country's flag). The approach is reminiscent of the laws of association of proximity in time and place that were studied extensively in psychology about a century ago (Woodworth & Schlosberg, 1954). At that time, associations were seen as connections between elements coincidental in time or place in a person's experiences. In contrast, the tenet of dynamic constructivism and priming research in cultural psychology is that the switches triggered by primes are associated with broad changes in psychological functioning, notably from an individualist to a collectivist orientation or vice versa (Oyserman & Lee, 2008). Thus, cultural frame switching implies broad generalizations (see the discussion on levels of generalizability in Section 2.3). Priming as a manipulation technique has been the subject of extensive debate (e.g., Doyen et al., 2012) and (the few) cross-cultural priming studies included in a major replication project have shown poor replicability (Klein et al., 2018; see Section 3.4).

In the past twenty years, many researchers in the schools of cultural psychology and cross-cultural psychology have become less adversarial about one another's research and theoretical perspectives and have started to emphasize common interests and complementarity of approaches (e.g., Cohen & Kitayama, 2019; Dasen & Mishra, 2010; Van de Vijver, Chasiotis, & Breugelmans, 2011). Complementarity continues to be questioned by researchers who identify with the label "sociocultural psychology." Historically speaking, they can lay claim to the name "cultural psychology" (*Kulturpsychologie* in German) more than the contemporary schools of (mainly North American) cultural psychology and of cross-cultural psychology. The tradition of sociocultural psychology explicitly traces its history back to the nineteenth century and concepts such as *Volksseele* (German for "soul of a people") or *Volksgeist* (German for "spirit of a people"). These concepts refer to a mode of psychological functioning transcending the individual. The central historical figure is Wundt (1913). He was not only the father of experimental psychology but also the author or a ten-volume treatise on *Völkerpsychologie* ("psychology of peoples"). The leading idea was that higher mental functions depend on collectives of humans and their cooperation (Jahoda & Krewer, 1997). Sociocultural psychology covers a broad range of ideas and topics, such as intentionality (Wen & Wang, 2013) and social representations (Moscovici, 1984) that are studied with a variety of methods (Rosa & Valsiner, 2018; Valsiner, 2012); this variation by itself already preempts a common definition of "culture."

The present overview is limited. Other orientations on culture and psychology might be mentioned, such as cultural historical activity theory, developed by Cole (e.g., 1996), where "culture" is not a given or a medium that can serve to explain differences in human behavior, but a state of affairs that needs to be explained. Several traditions not covered here tend to be non-comparative and holistic and to expand into disciplines such as education, philosophy, parts of linguistics, and cultural anthropology. The work of Bruner (e.g., 1990) can serve as an entry point to such approaches that are broader, and in many respects richer, than thinking in (c)cp as presented here. However, these approaches are hardly open to validation with methods that are independent of the person of the researcher (see Section 3).

2.1.1 Biological Anchoring

Schools in (c)cp predominantly started from a social science orientation that paid little attention to the biological anchoring of human behavior. Researchers generally aligned with cultural anthropology and largely avoided seeking inspiration from comparative psychology, physical anthropology, or ethology. Using the term "sociobiology," Wilson (1975) explained human social behavior within an evolutionary framework. This left space only for minor population differences in human psychological functioning and initially met with great resistance. Sahlins (1977) argued pointedly that these "small margins" leave a void in which the whole of anthropology fits. Ethologists like

Goodall (e.g., 1986), famous for her studies of chimpanzees in their natural settings, and de Waal (2008), who observed captive colonies of chimpanzees and later bonobos, have shown that psychological traits and processes, like emotions, cooperation, and even deceit, are not features of only the human species. Moreover, ethologists have demonstrated in several species of mammals and birds the transmission of learned actions across generations. Much of the evidence comes from studies meeting high methodological standards, virtually ruling out any alternative explanation (such as spontaneous occurrence). For example, Aplin et al. (2015) taught a few great tits a technique to open a puzzle box containing highly preferred food. This technique spread rapidly in groups of these birds and was found to be transmitted over generations. A strong point in the evidence is that two versions of the technique were taught to individual birds belonging to different groups and that in each group the version that had been taught to some of its members persisted.

An important aspect of this theorizing are mathematical models of transmission, which allow for formalization and precision. Cavalli-Sforza and Feldman (1981) modeled the diffusion of specific technological inventions and diseases in recorded history, drawing parallels with processes of genetic evolution. They emphasized a distinction between (i) vertical transmission from parent to offspring, (ii) horizontal transmission between (often unrelated) members of the same generation, and (iii) oblique transmission between members of one generation to members of another generation who are not their descendants. It should be noted that Cavalli-Sforza and Feldman addressed well-defined phenomena. For many traits of human behavior, the phylogenetic history is unknown; attempts at reconstruction then easily become speculative.

A question relevant for the present discussion is whether biologically based theorizing known as cultural evolution theories, can advance the conceptualization of "culture" for (c)cp. A well-known formulation is the dual inheritance theory of Boyd and Richerson (1985). This theory explicitly postulates two forms of inheritance: genetic inheritance operating through genetic transmission from one generation to the next and cultural inheritance based on social learning. In their view, imitation (in the sense of Bandura, 1977), conformity to group rules, and prestige seeking are mechanisms in the adaptation and diffusion of practices. However, it needs to be emphasized that the two systems are not at an equal level: genetic inheritance largely determines the boundaries of the space of affordances for human behavior variations (see Section 4.1.2). Richerson and Boyd (2005, p. 5) provide a formal definition of "culture" as "information capable of affecting individuals' behavior that they acquire from other members of their species through teaching, imitation, and other forms 'of social transmission." Mesoudi et al. (2006, p. 331) endorse this definition, adding "'Information' is employed as a broad term incorporating ideas, knowledge, beliefs, values, skills, and attitudes." It may be noted that such broad formulations are not very helpful in trying to specify more precisely what is being transmitted. For example, Mesoudi et al. (2006) write about "cultural traits" but are unclear about what these entail (see Fuentes, 2006; Lyman, 2006). The same difficulty pertains to notions about units of cultural transmission paralleling genes in biological transmission, such as "memes" proposed originally by Dawkins (1976) or "culture genes" proposed by Lumsden and Wilson (1981).

It has been recognized that more intricate arguments are needed to make "culture" (in nonhuman animals) accessible to critical research. Whiten (2021, p. 212) has suggested "decompos[ing] culture into aspects such as (a) the ways in which traditions are distributed in space and time, (b) the underlying learning processes, and (c) the behavioral or other specific contents of the traditions." According to Whiten, the "real science" (quotation marks in the original) can begin when a researcher has provided an explicit definition of the phenomenon at stake. It appears to me that there are two ways to go: (i) specify what is meant by "culture" in any particular instance where the term is used or (ii) avoid the term in research, as suggested in this Element. I would argue that the latter choice is more parsimonious and avoids fuzzy connotations; however, with strict definitions the two options are not far apart. In contrast to meticulous considerations as mentioned by Whiten, many behavioral ecologists and ethologists appear to use the term "culture" almost as easily as researchers in (c)cp, and, despite formal theorizing about behavior transmission and strict methods in addressing the target behavior of a study, most of their conceptualizations of "culture" remain vague. Often, the concept tends to be invoked as a kind of *deus ex machina* (i.e., supernatural intervention in ancient Greek plays to solve intractable problems).

2.2 "A Culture"

"Culture," whatever the term may imply, is seen as being shared by the members of some population. Such a population is called "a culture." In early cultural anthropology, an ethnography provided an analysis of a more or less isolated population and covered major parts of the behavior repertoire. In such ethnographies, the notion of "a culture" presumed substantial differentiation (differences with other populations) and permanence (continuity over time) (Berry et al., 2011). This original meaning has been expanded and has become fuzzier in various ways. Nowadays, "a culture" can also refer to a temporary grouping of individuals within a society, as in "youth culture" or "organization culture."

There can be salient characteristics of membership (dress, body ornaments), but many groupings are lacking permanence and membership often affects only a very limited part of the behavior repertoire. In (c)cp, "a culture" most often refers to a country or global region. Nationals of various countries tend to show clear differences on a range of external context variables, including climate, language, affluence, or political organization, as well as a host of customs and practices. Such national populations, in many respects, reasonably meet conditions of differentiation and permanence.

Major fields of study in (c)cp where permanence and differentiation become problematic are intercultural relations and acculturation. Migrants may follow different acculturation strategies (Berry 1997) and receiving societies impose different pressures (Bourhis et al., 1997). With a range of acculturation trajectories and large numbers of people moving and settling temporarily across borders (migrants, sojourners, refugees), increasingly complex interactions patterns have to be accounted for (see also Section 5.2). Neighborhoods in large cities have inhabitants originating from dozens of countries. New terms have been coined. "Superdiversity" refers to communities with large variations in home languages and ethnic and national origins (Van de Vijver et al., 2015; Vertovec, 2007). "Polycultural psychology" points to multiple influences on individuals (Morris, Chiu, & Liu, 2015). "Culture mixing" refers to the simultaneous presence of symbols from different origin in the same space and time (Hao et al., 2016).

Morris et al. (2015) describe individuals' relationships to "cultures" as partial and plural rather than categorical. At the same time, these authors appear to attribute system-like properties to "culture" with their definition: "a loosely integrated system of ideas, practices, and social institutions that enables coordination of behavior in a population" (p. 632). Frame switching allows "biculturals' experience of switching cultural lenses from one transitory situation to the next" (p. 638). However, it is difficult to imagine how the behavior of people in modern urban environments who may have been born in country A, studied in country B, and work and live in country C can be partitioned and attributed to these various backgrounds. It is even less clear which notion should be applied to members of superdiverse societies or communities. With increasing mobility, the complexity of interconnections between "cultural systems" becomes staggering, and critical analysis within the model of polycultural psychology becomes unrealistic.

There are signs of researchers moving away from the central position of "cultural" descent and toward the actual context of interaction. For example, researchers in social geography examine current contact and interaction in different settings (Wilson, 2017). Location is also central in research on the spatial distribution of psychological traits by Rentfrow and colleagues (e.g., Rentfrow & Jokela 2016). In a survey with samples from several (affluent) countries, the Pew Research Center (2017) found that speaking the national language was seen more frequently as important for national identity (to be one of "us") than country of origin. Another trend is research defining and comparing populations in terms of some specific feature. An example is segmentation in international marketing research, whereby the focus is on (sub)populations defined in common terms across countries, such as levels of income (Steenkamp & Ter Hofstede, 2002). In my reading, these developments do not mean that comparative analysis of behavior in human populations will become less important but that in future populations will be defined in differentiated and, one may hope, more precise terms than currently is the case when they are referred to as "cultures."

2.3 Inferences from Data

In (c)cp, data collected from more than one population are the basis for inferences or interpretations of how the populations concerned differ in respect to some underlying psychological characteristic. The kinds of interpretations they make reflect how researchers conceptualize these differences (Poortinga, 2003). Generalizability Theory (Cronbach et al., 1972) provides a point of entry. In this theory, a set of stimuli or a set of items forming a scale is seen as a sample of the entire collection of elements that belong to a domain of generalization. (Cronbach and colleagues refer to a "universe of generalization"; in (c)cp the term "domain of generalization" is more common.) The theory emphasizes that the same data can be interpreted in various ways; that is, they can be generalized to various domains. For example, scores on a test of arithmetic can be generalized to the level of skills (some children perform better in arithmetic than others do), to the level of the aptitude to learn arithmetic (some children are more gifted than others are), or to the quality of education in schools (as happens in the PISA studies of the OECD, www.oecd.org/pisa/aboutpisa/). Any generalization presumes that the elements making up a domain belong together in some essential way; in other words, within a domain there is coherence. To illustrate the implications, a distinction is made here between between three levels of generalization: (i) unconstrained or poorly constrained hypothetical domains, (ii) hypothetical domains open to analysis of construct validity, and (iii) domains for which there is agreement in a population about which elements belong (i.e., domains characterized by high content validity).

The conceptualization of "a-culture-as-a-system" (e.g., a system of meanings or a network of representations) includes the entire behavior repertoire, or at least a major part, and amounts to a very broad generalization; in a system, all elements are interrelated. A telling illustration is a statement by Geertz that "a culture" is neither like a pile of loose sand nor neatly organized as a spider's web; it is "more like an octopus, a badly integrated creature – what passes for a brain keeps it together, more or less, in one ungainly whole" (cited by Shweder, 1984, p. 19). The formulation of this metaphor may suggest otherwise, but it implies very strong coherence; every part of the octopus is connected closely to every other part. This kind of presumed coherence is characteristic of theorizing in classical ethnography where a cultural system tends to be portrayed as integrated and also as unique for the population concerned. As indicated earlier, there is no agreed upon set of organizational principles or parameters in terms of which such a system can be described; widely accepted flow diagrams or organizational charts are not to be found. Consequently, generalization to a cultural system amounts to an interpretation that is beyond critical empirical analysis. Generalizations to poorly constrained domains typical for (c)cp are dichotomies such as the East versus West dichotomy covering social and cognitive functioning, and dimensions such as individualism-collectivism. As mentioned in Section 1.5, these distinctions are associated with broad and poorly demarcated swaths of behavior. The attractiveness of broad domains is parsimoniousness; each dichotomy or dimension potentially has a wide explanatory reach. However, broad domains are fuzzy; it is not clear what belongs and what does not belong. As a result, explanations are loose and imprecise, and they escape analysis geared toward validation and falsification.

Typical for the second category are generalizations from scores on inventories and questionnaires to hypothetical constructs, such as personality traits, cognitive abilities, emotions, and values. Such generalizations are in principle open to analysis of construct validity across populations (an important caveat is that measurements are possibly biased or lacking equivalence; this psychometric concern is taken up in Section 3.3.2). Research on personality traits may illustrate how analysis can progress over time. The Five Factor Model that has been dominant in the literature for a few decades postulates five dimensions: extraversion, neuroticism, openness to experience, conscientiousness, and agreeableness. In studies with the Neo-PI-R, the inventory most widely used for assessment, the five-dimensional structure has been replicated across a wide range of countries (McCrae et al., 2005). However, results obtained with local personality inventories developed in China (Cheung et al., 1996) and in South Africa (Nel et al., 2012), strongly suggested that orientation on interpersonal relations is underrepresented in the FFM. When these inventories subsequently were administered in other populations, such as Western students, the factor structures were found to replicate quite well, including the interpersonal relations factor (Cheung et al., 2006; Valchev et al., 2014). Thus, it appears that for a given inventory, the factor structure of personality traits is similar, at least across literate societies, but that this structure varies depending on the choice of inventory (Church, 2016). The string of studies mentioned shows how at this level of generalization accumulation of research may reveal limitations in accepted findings and progressively lead to better knowledge.

At the third level, one generalizes from data to fields of behavior defined in terms of knowledge, skills, or attitudes or some category of situations. Usually, it is clear which elements belong to such a domain, and a test or questionnaire can be developed representing the domain. At this level, domains may well differ in behavior content across populations (e.g., skills in arithmetical operations such as root extraction are basically absent in nonliterate societies). However, it should be possible to identify discrepancies and reach content validity for any population. If discrepancies are not evident from the start (e.g., a researcher fails to realize that root extraction is not taught in some curriculum), they should emerge from analysis of equivalence and cultural bias (see Section 3.3.2). In other words, it can be made clear for any element whether or not it belongs to the specified domain.

This reasoning can also be applied to domains defined in terms of categories of situations and referred to with terms such as "customs," "habits," or "practices." In this Element, the term "conventions" is used, implying agreement in a population about how something ought to be done or ought to be thought of. There is an aspect of arbitrariness to conventions; at the same time having or not having a convention on how to deal with a certain situation may not be at all arbitrary. (The iconic example is that it does not matter much whether there is right-hand or left-hand traffic in a country, while it is essential that all cars stick to the same side of the road.) Conventions are not limited to overt actions; they include beliefs, ways to handle problems (e.g., preference for wooden houses over stone houses, or vice versa), and explanations or justifications of conventions (e.g., reasons why wooden houses are better). Conspicuous examples include greeting rituals and display rules for emotions. In view of their large number, conventions can be equated with the words in a dictionary. Translations of words with the help of a dictionary are likely to go wrong on shades of meaning. There are analogous mismatches with conventions; misunderstandings and misinterpretations in intercultural communication are notorious (Girndt & Poortinga, 1997).

At this low level of generalization, striking differences in behavior with enormous consequences can be found, depending on how information or an action is categorized. An extreme example is abortion. In societies where a fetus is seen as a human being, abortion may be classified as murder; elsewhere it is considered to be a woman's right to make decisions about her own body. Conventions can have a long lifetime; an obvious example are scripts and the direction of writing that in some cases have passed from generation to generation over millennia. Also, religious beliefs (dealing with the transcendent and beyond reality testing) can be particularly resistant to change. Conventions can have unexpected consequences; for example, the grammatical gender of object names in languages like Spanish and German has an effect on the rates of associations with more feminine or more masculine characteristics (Boroditsky et al., 2003). However, broader implications for the world view of the speakers of these languages are highly unlikely (see McWhorter, 2014).

In summary, the core question with generalizability is whether various differences in manifest behavior between populations that happen to coexist can be interpreted as psychologically related. Coincidence (phenomena just co-occurring) and coherence (phenomena being related psychologically) have to be distinguished carefully.

2.4 Conclusion

The argument in this section suggests that for psychological research geared to testing hypotheses about behavior differences, the concept of "culture" is too vague. If so, it should not be used in such research (Poortinga, 2015). Avoiding the defining concept of "culture" in (c)cp may look revolutionary but only amounts to precise definition of research targets. Concepts, including central concepts in a scientific discipline, can become obsolete or change over time. In physics, "ether" has disappeared as a medium carrying light waves in a vacuum. In biology, *generatio spontanea* has been left behind as a principle through which complete organisms appear spontaneously, such as frogs from mud and vermin from decaying material. Today psychology is still named after the concept of *psyche* (soul), even though behavior (overt and covert) has become the field of study. There is no reason why "culture" in (c)cp should be exempt from major change. The perspective taken here is that social functioning in groups can be conceptualized as based in the individual person. We are social beings because we are equipped individually to resonate and coordinate our actions with others. Features of individual functioning such as "mirror neurons" (Iacoboni, 2009) and hormones (e.g., oxytocin) preempt the need for "psychological" concepts transcending the individual, such as social representations or collective emotions.

The need for precision also pertains to the definition of populations in (c)cp. By attaching the label "culture" to all kinds of groupings, criteria of differentiation and demarcation have been relaxed greatly. With the kind of reasoning outlined here, populations need to be clearly distinct, but they need to be defined in terms of specific variables or behavior domains rather than in terms of some poorly defined part of the behavior repertoire.

A problematic aspect of conceptualization in (c)cp is the level of generalizability of observed differences between populations. The most salient differences are found in small domains, here referred to as conventions. A few examples have illustrated how the way in which some event or situation is classified can have major consequences. When moving from conventions to increasingly larger domains of generalization, psychological differences between populations tend to become smaller and their validity more difficult to demonstrate.

3 Method

This section first describes the notion of the empirical cycle as a way to transcend the contrast between quantitative and qualitative research that has been a major theme in (c)cp for a long time. In the next two subsections, difficulties with both qualitative and quantitative methodology are discussed. In addition, attention is paid to a general concern in need of urgent attention, namely a frequently found lack of replicability and an associated need for preregistration of studies.

3.1 The Empirical Cycle

A venerable distinction in the scientific process is that between a context of discovery, or exploration, and a context of verification, or confirmation. According to Reichenbach (1938), discovery is of little interest; science is about verification. In logical positivism, a dominant school of philosophy at the time, a leading question was how to examine and verify the truth of an empirical statement. This question was uprooted by Popper (1959), who argued that such statements never can be fully verified and that researchers should seek falsification rather than verification. An example is the observation of black ravens. Even if we have observed many ravens that all were black, this logically does not rule out that we can come across some non-black raven in the future. Although criticized later on (e.g., Kuhn, 1962; Lakatos, 1974), Popper's epistemological principles, often referred to as "post-positivism," are still widely accepted in psychological research. The idea is that a true state of affairs may never be known with absolute certainty, but it can be approximated; for example, until some raven is found with another color, it makes sense to expect that the next raven that we come across will be black. There are alternative epistemological views, such as constructivism (e.g., Gergen, 1985). This view challenges the idea of a reality out there that can be known and considers knowledge as being constructed in interactions with others through hermeneutical and dialectical methods (e.g., unstructured interviews and focus groups). For (c)cp. this implies that pursuing a single psychology for all humankind is misguided; there can only be multiple indigenous psychologies.

This major divide is associated with quantitative and qualitative research traditions and in (c)cp can be seen as the epistemological side of the relativism-universalism debate discussed in Section 2.1. The school of cross-cultural psychology emerged at a time when views from logical positivism were still common, and psychometric tests and experiments had become the standard methods of scientific psychology. Indigenous and early culturalist traditions, following a qualitative methodology, were an almost unavoidable reaction against positivist doctrine. In turn, embracing relativism may have been an overly strong reaction, too frequently amounting to "a flight from science and reason" (Gross et al., 1996).

The viewpoint in this Element is that in the end, the contrast between qualitative and quantitative research is not a fruitful dichotomy and that these two orientations are best seen as complementary in a continuing process of discovery and justification. According to De Groot (see De Groot & Spiekerman, 1969), scientific research proceeds through an empirical cycle with five stages: *observation – induction – deduction – testing – evaluation*. In the observation phase, available information is organized and conjectures are formulated. In the induction phase, hypotheses are specified – tentative explanations from which consequences can be derived that are open to empirical examination. In the deduction phase, concepts are operationalized in methods, so that the hypotheses are open for measurement, allowing specific predictions about measurement outcomes. In the testing phase, the hypotheses are confronted with such outcomes, and it is decided whether or not the predictions have been met. In the final evaluation phase, the findings are interpreted, with a view to the strength of competing theories and the need for further investigation, which amounts to starting a new cycle. The precise definition and demarcation of the phases do not require elaboration here; what matters is that the empirical cycle, in (c)cp as elsewhere, begins with analyses more characteristic of qualitative methodology and ends with kinds of analysis more attuned to quantitative methodology.

3.2 Qualitative Research

A major strength of qualitative research is the richness of descriptive data gathered with flexible methods, such as open interviews, focus groups, and the observation of events as they occur or are reported retrospectively by informers. Triangulation of data gained from various sources and through various methods strengthens interpretation. The collection of data is not harnessed by standardized methods, such as fixed items sets and Likert response scales. Rather, methods are selected that are available to address the question at hand; methodology is meant to help identify complex phenomena hidden in unstructured data.

Among researchers preferring a qualitative orientation, views on interpretation differ substantially. Some authors insist that their interpretations are valid; careful data collection and sensitive analysis more or less guarantee validity in the sense of rendering the true meaning of what participants report (see, e.g., Bryman, 2015). Most authors demand evidence of "trustworthiness." For example, Guba (1981) and Schwandt et al. (2007) put forward a specific terminology for qualitative research to replace conventional quantitative terms: credibility (for internal validity), transferability (for external validity), dependability (for reliability), and confirmability (for objectivity). A wide range of methods and techniques are available to strengthen a research process (e.g., Bryman, 2015; Creswell, 2009). For example, in semi-structured interviews, interactions are guided by a prepared list of topics to ensure that all relevant aspects are covered, while opportunities for spontaneous elaborations by the interviewee remain. A research design can specify that "saturation" has to be reached; that is, interviewing or focus group sessions are continued until hardly any novel information is forthcoming. The coding of data, which is at the core of the analysis process, can be supported by coding schemes that help uncover phenomena hidden in the data. Corbin and Strauss (1990) distinguished three types of coding: (i) open coding (giving conceptual labels and categorizing phenomena), (ii) axial coding (relating categories and subcategories), and (iii) selective coding (integration of all categories in a core category). Nowadays coding tends to be done with the help of computer programs, such as Atlas.ti (www.atlasti.com) that follow such a sequence.

Integration of qualitative and quantitative approaches is reflected in "mixed methods." Most common is a qualitative project phase followed by a quantitative phase (Creswell, 2009; Karasz, 2011). In the qualitative phase, a topic is explored, constructs may be formulated, and hypotheses generated. In the quantitative phase, the hypotheses are tested statistically. The order of the phases is reversed when qualitative methods are used to follow up on quantitative findings, for example, to find out why an intervention does not work or in (c)cp why a previously established relation between variables is not found in some other population. One specific illustration of a qualitative phase in the development and use of quantitative psychometric instruments in c(c)p is the analysis of observed item bias with the help of cognitive interviews. Informants are asked how they understand and interpret items, in order to explain population differences in item score distributions (Benítez et al., 2018; Karasz, 2011).

From the perspective of scientific research as an empirical cycle, the main strength of qualitative methods is the openness to new and unexpected information, and the main weakness is the lack of controls on validity that are independent of the person of the researcher. In the view of researchers oriented toward quantitative methodology, claims to empirical validity become questionable when the person of the researcher is central to all phases of the empirical cycle, including testing and evaluation – that is, when researchers serve as their own instruments.

3.3 Quantitative Methodology

The methodological principles for research in psychology apply equally in (c) cp, but some issues are more salient. Stimuli (items) and responses are likely to be biased, leading to non-equivalent results. In addition, participants invariably are nested in populations, with consequences for sampling and data analysis. Perhaps a more general concern is that in (c)cp there is a strong tendency toward seeking convergent evidence and ignoring concerns about discriminant evidence (Campbell & Fiske, 1959). The consequences have been illustrated in Section 1, and they will emerge again in the discussion on replicability (see Section 3.4).

3.3.1 Selection of Populations and Samples

Sampling in (c)cp pertains to selection of populations and to selection of individuals nested within each population. The parameters on which populations are to be selected depend on the question that is examined. The number of populations needs to be large enough to allow reasonably precise estimates of statistics, for example, in structural equation models (e.g., Selig, Card, & Little, 2008). Campbell (1964) long ago warned that two-group comparisons are highly vulnerable to effects of confounding variables. Unless there is a strong theory allowing precise operationalization and measurement, such comparisons should be avoided. Even with larger numbers of populations, there is the threat of confounding variables; for example, in studies seeking worldwide representation, Western and high-income countries tend to be overrepresented, usually with unknown consequences.

Sampling of individual participants within populations often happens on an ad hoc basis. In an overview of the literature, Boehnke et al. (2011) found convenience sampling (such as a class of students at some university to represent the population of a country) for more than half of a set of studies that were examined. These authors note an important point: for studies not aiming at differences in levels of scores but only at relations between variables, a sample of "typical" members of a population rather than a randomly selected sample may be sufficient, as precise distributions of score levels are not relevant. Of course, the question remains when a sample can be said to consist of "typical" members. The proportion of young people entering university or another form of tertiary-level education varies across countries from a few percentage points to well over one-third of an age cohort. Unfortunately, it is difficult to guess how much discrepancy there may be between the actual results obtained with a given selection procedure and the results that would have been obtained with a randomly selected sample of participants. Samples that are representative of the target populations are worth an effort to obtain them.

3.3.2 Equivalence and Bias in Data

Quantitative methods hinge on standardized instruments, observation schedules, and experimental procedures for data collection that result in quantifiable scores. A major concern in (c)cp is that differences between populations in score distributions or in relationships between score variables should not be interpreted at face value. Various sources of bias can lead to "lack of comparability" or "lack of equivalence," that is, unequal representation of the domain of generalization (e.g., Bender & Adams, 2021; Boer et al., 2018; Van de Vijver & Leung, 1997, 2021).

It is important to distinguish between forms of bias, such as construct bias, method bias, and item bias (Van de Vijver & Leung, 2021; Van de Vijver & Poortinga, 1997). *Item bias* occurs when testees from different populations with the same overall score on an instrument do not have the same probability of giving a certain answer to a certain item. Poor item translation appears to be the most frequent cause of item bias. *Method bias* refers to misrepresentation of differences in a domain of generalization resulting from some shared characteristic of the items in an instrument or the way it is administered. Sources of method bias include modes of instruction, response styles (acquiescence, extreme responding) and social desirability (He et al., 2014), and effects of the reference group in terms of which respondents evaluate themselves (Heine et al., 2002). Differences due to method bias are difficult to differentiate from valid differences, as this form of bias tends to affect all items in a scale to a similar extent. *Construct bias* occurs when a set of items does not equally represent the domain of generalization across populations. For example, parental affiliation (concern for elderly parents) presumably is found everywhere.

Items asking about economic support (e.g., do respondents intend to have their aging parents live with them) may reflect parental affiliation in a traditional society. Items asking about social support (e.g., visits to elderly parents and telephone calls) may be indicative of affiliation in a contemporary urban society (Georgas et al., 2006).

The presence of bias in a data set does not necessarily preclude all forms of comparison; much depends on which interpretation researchers want to derive from the data and which psychometric properties of score variables are affected. It is customary to distinguish four levels of equivalence or psychometric invariance (Fontaine, 2005). *Construct equivalence*, the first level, implies identity of a construct, independent of the question of whether or not it cannot be operationalized or measured in the same way across populations. *Structural equivalence*, the second level, is satisfied when there are isomorphic (order-preserving) relationships between variables across populations. To examine structural relationships, correlational techniques are used (such as multidimensional scaling for ordinal data and factor analysis for data with interval scale properties). *Metric equivalence*, or *measurement unit equivalence*, the third level, is satisfied when units of measurement are equal across populations (i.e., equal distances on a scoring scale across populations represent equal distances in standing in the domain of generalization). The fourth and final level is *full score equivalence*. When this level of invariance is met, a score of a given value can be interpreted in the same way across populations. In other words, direct comparison of individual scores obtained in distinct populations presumes full score equivalence. In the past, analyses were based mostly on observed score variables; now the focus is more on latent variables and structural equation modeling. Three levels of equivalence or psychometric invariance tend to be distinguished: (i) configural invariance (corresponding to structural equivalence), (ii) metric invariance (corresponding to metric equivalence), and (iii) scalar invariance (corresponding to full score equivalence) (Byrne & Van de Vijver, 2010).

There are complications with the analysis of equivalence. In large data sets, psychometric criteria for fit are hardly ever met, as even a slight bias effect will lead to a statistically significant lack of equivalence. Recently, analysis procedures have been proposed that allow relaxation of criteria for equivalence (see Boer et al., 2018, for an overview). Another complication is that various approaches used for item bias analysis (also called "differential item functioning" or DIF) do not always identify the same items as biased (Fortin Morales et al., 2013). However, most worrisome is that possible bias in data often is not examined at all. Boer et al. (2018) have shown that in a majority of studies in cross-cultural research, issues of bias and lack of equivalence are not discussed, implying that authors assume that the required level of equivalence for a given interpretation is met by their data. Such an assumption is hard to justify in view of the extensive evidence on the presence of bias.

3.3.3 Design Issues

The remainder of this section assumes that experiments offer a powerful method to differentiate between findings that are less likely and findings that are more likely to be valid representations of reality. The experimental method is geared to the later phases of the empirical cycle – testing of hypotheses and evaluation of outcomes. Its strength lies in the specification of principles for causal inference from data (see Shadish, Cook, & Campbell, 2002, chap. 14, for the rationale of this viewpoint). A true experiment meets two requirements: the experimenter has control over the treatments that are administered to subjects/ participants and control over their assignment to the various treatment conditions. Control over a treatment implies that the experimenter can manipulate the treatment conditions and there is little variance due to uncontrolled variables (confounding variables). In (c)cp, differences in "treatments" are associated with differences between "cultures" and often are extremely vague. To meet the second condition, subjects/participants have to be assigned randomly to treatments; in this way, effects of possible confounding factors are minimized. Experiments in which subjects are nested in treatment conditions and thus not assigned randomly are called "quasi-experiments." Typical examples are found in education research, when classrooms or schools are the unit of selection rather than individual pupils, and in organizational research, when teams of workers are the unit of selection (Shadish et al., 2002). For research in (c)cp with global regions or countries as units of selection, the extent of prior differences in background, and thus of uncontrolled variables (potential confounds), is large. Consequently, it is difficult to reasonably meet conditions for quasi-experimental designs.

Threats to erroneous interpretation in (quasi-)experimental research do not only come from uncertainty about the fit of the data to the usual model of null-hypothesis statistical testing (NHST). Concerns have increasingly been raised about choices that researchers make during the various stages of a study (e.g., Ioannides, 2005). Simmons et al. (2011) refer to such choices as "academic degrees of freedom." They warn against "false-positive psychology" where "flexibility in data collection, analysis, and reporting dramatically increases actual false-positive rates. In many cases, a researcher is more likely to falsely find evidence that an effect exists than to correctly find evidence that it does not" (p. 1359).

Various frequently found transgressions of methodological standards have been identified. Cohen (1994) has warned against the interpretation of a high level of "statistical" significance as evidence of a "big and important" difference. Button et al. (2013) have emphasized that with small samples, more than with large samples, there is not only a smaller probability of detecting a true effect but also a larger probability that an observed statistically significant result does not reflect a true effect (see the example of fMRI studies in Section 1.6). Other poor practices relate to "p-hacking," the search for and emphasis on significant differences in designs with multiple variables, and to "harking," adding hypotheses after results are known (Wicherts et al., 2016). There have been suggestions to abandon the terminology "p < .05" and statistical significance or to replace the NHST model by Bayesian statistical analysis. The main differences with NHST are that parameters are not fixed and that prior information can be taken into account (Van de Schoot et al., 2014). It is important to realize that such an alternative statistical method is not immune to most of the errors and implicit manipulations of results just mentioned. Whatever statistical analysis procedure is chosen, for the logic behind the experiment, there does not appear to be a ready alternative.

3.3.4 Individual-Level and Population-Level Analysis

In designs with individuals nested in populations, multilevel analysis is needed to tease apart the two levels, because a shift in level may require a shift in explanatory concept (Van de Vijver, Van Hemert, & Poortinga, 2008). For example, across populations, the average number of color words known by children will depend on the number of color words in their language. Within a linguistic population, differences between children will also reflect their individual knowledge. In this example, the generalizations of the scores at the two levels are to unrelated concepts, that is, the vocabulary of a language and the verbal skills of children.

The question is whether individual scores and country scores are "isomorphic" (i.e., whether there is a monotonic function describing the relationship between the scores at the two levels) and whether the scores at both levels are interpretable in terms of identical constructs. This is examined best by analyzing whether the structure of the interrelationships between variables (usually questionnaire items) is the same at the two levels (Hox, 2010). Since for stable estimates, data from numerous countries are needed, existing empirical evidence on (non)isomorphism is limited. For the Schwartz Value Survey (SVS), Fischer et al. (2010) found substantial similarity in structure across levels, although statistical indices were not high enough to support full structural isomorphism. In a discussion typical for a field where differences are emphasized, these authors pursued possible reasons for the slightly less than perfect isomorphism. In another study, Fischer and Poortinga (2012) concluded that a single configuration provides a good representation of individual and national value structures.

In an extensive study on self-construal showing a seven-dimensional model of self-construal (or selfhood), Vignoles et al. (2016) found that statistical criteria for structural isomorphism were met if results for a few items were removed from the data set. Further evidence suggests that the Big Five personality dimensions (McCrae & Terraciano, 2008) and subjective well-being (Lucas & Diener, 2008; Van Hemert et al., 2002) apply to countries as well as to individuals. Although more large-scale studies are needed to reach firm conclusions, the findings mentioned suggest that psychological traits, such as social values and personality dimensions, make sense (i.e., have construct validity) at both the level of individuals and the level of countries. In short, just as individuals can differ in how happy or extraverted they are, populations can be said to differ in the level of happiness or extraversion.

3.4 Replication and Preregistration

For a long time, novel research was considered more original and was easier to publish than replications (why rehash what is known already?). This attitude is changing, because large replicability projects have shown alarmingly poor results. In one recent project in psychology, fewer than 40 percent of the 100 included studies were successfully replicated (Open Science Collaboration, 2015). In another large-scale effort, replicating each of twenty-eight studies about sixty times across thirty-six countries and territories, just over half of the original effects were supported (Klein et al., 2018). For the three studies from the domain of (c)cp included in the project reported by Klein et al. (viz., Huang et al., 2014, Study 1; Miyamoto & Kitayama, 2002; Norenzayan et al., 2002), the original differences were not replicated. Also noteworthy is that for studies in the set of twenty-eight for which the results did replicate, findings were similar for Western and non-Western countries. This evidence suggests that differences between populations on typical psychological constructs tend to be small and underlines a strong need for research in (c)cp to anchor claims about differences between populations securely in sound methods.

When replications challenge the findings of original studies, their authors are apt to point to changes in research protocols as the reason for discrepancies. This point is noted here explicitly as replication of research in (c)cp is not straightforward (see Milfont & Klein, 2018, for a review). The transfer of methods across populations often requires some kind of adaptation of these methods. This can include translation, replacement of items in psychometric scales, or changes in administration (paper and pencil vs. online) (Van de Vijver & Poortinga, 2020). Such adaptations are likely to affect psychometric equivalence, and researchers have to ask themselves whether a lack of replicability could be due to less than perfect adaptation. Lykken (1968) has made a distinction between literal replication, where exactly the same method has to be followed, and constructive replication, where only essential features are to be retained. Research in (c)cp is largely limited to constructive replication, especially when populations that differ substantially in overt behavior repertoires are involved.

Under these conditions, a major step toward strengthening research in (c)cp is preregistration, that is, registration before data are collected of the theoretical background, design, hypotheses, and procedures of a study in an open register, such as www.AsPredicted.org. Also, an increasing number of journals are considering preregistered reports – detailed research proposals that are reviewed before data collection. If accepted, publication of the study after completion is guaranteed, regardless of the outcomes, as long as the authors follow their preregistered data collection and analysis plan. Preregistration increases transparency and strongly limits "academic degrees of freedom." There is no restriction on post hoc interpretation of unexpected findings, but discrepancies between expectations and outcomes are explicit. Preregistration does not impose restrictions on the design of studies; it is also possible for qualitative studies (Haven & Van Grootel, 2019). If researchers adhering to discrepant theories design a study together, this approach allows the direct testing of competing hypotheses (Ellemers et al., 2020). Pregistration is not a magic wand; it slows down the research process, and unavoidable adaptations of the original plans may become problematic (Nosek et al., 2018). However, changes in a study are made transparently, and there is a clear distinction between predicted findings and post hoc interpretation. In principle, preregistration can deal with many of the methodological issues raised in this section.

3.5 Conclusion

Piecemeal small studies conducted by individual researchers, whether following qualitative or quantitative methodologies, may not be viable much longer. Plausibility (or validity) of interpretation of findings is a problem with qualitative research. With quantitative studies, the prior probability of observing some difference and rejection of the 0-hypothesis of no difference can be so high (p $\gg$ .05) that they become virtually meaningless (Malpass & Poortinga, 1986).

So far, the replicability crisis has had limited impact on (c)cp; however, there is little reason to assume that we are doing better than neighboring fields of research, such as experimental social psychology, and that we can continue to avoid strict requirements of accountability.

Thus, there is a challenge to improve methodology in (c)cp. A first step is to conduct more carefully designed projects with controls on confounding variables, systematic analysis of data and a sharp distinction between predicted outcomes and post hoc interpretation (see Fischer& Poortinga, 2018 for a listing of requirements). Extensive studies, with samples from numerous countries, are well known in (c)cp, but, so far, these are often focused on a lead idea or a particular instrument put forward by a senior (Western) researcher. For the future, research strategies are needed that start with an exploratory phase in each participating population and that lead to data deposits open for further analysis by other researchers. Projects with recurrent data collection, such as the large international studies on quality of school education of the OECD (known by their acronyms, PISA and TALIS www.oecd.org; Van de Vijver et al., 2019) and the European Values Study (www.europeanvaluesstudy.eu) have taken steps in this direction. The move toward open reproducible science and more representative research teams is only just starting.

4 Incorporating Development and Change

The lead question in this Element is how differences in behavior between human populations can be best analyzed and explained. In the previous sections, the focus was on the most frequently found research strategy in (c)cp, that is, mapping behavior differences between populations and linking such differences to antecedent conditions. In this section, the contours are sketched of a more comprehensive strategy addressing multiple questions simultaneously, following the ethologist Tinbergen (1963). He mentioned four questions to guide the analysis of behavior patterns: questions of causation, function, phylogenetic development, and ontogenetic development. A fifth question typical for human behavior is added here, namely the question of how changes in the course of historical time have influenced current patterns of behavior.

4.1 Tinbergen's Four Questions

Ethology, the study of behavior of nonhuman animals in their natural environment, gained prominence at a time when behaviorism with its emphasis on learning (conditioning, reinforcement) was a leading paradigm. A dominant question in ethology was how much of the behavior of an animal was "learned" and how much was "innate." The main method of study was observation of a species in its natural environment. In a foundational article, Tinbergen (1963) argued that four questions have to be answered in the analysis of a behavior pattern: (i) the mechanisms or causes of the behavior, (ii) the function it supposedly serves, (iii) its evolutionary history, and (iv) its ontogenetic development. There has been debate on the number of perspectives that should be distinguished and on their formulation (e.g., proximate causation vs. ultimate causation; Mayr, 1961), but the original four questions continue to be prominent (Bolhuis & Verhulst, 2009; Manning & Dawkins, 2012).

For various reasons, Tinbergen's questions can be considered relevant for (c) cp. First and foremost, ethologists tend to be interested in behavior processes, rather than in a target species. For (c)cp, a corresponding orientation would imply more emphasis on context-outcome relationships, and less on how populations differ from one another. In addition, (c)cp has important similarities with ethological research as it was conducted sixty years ago. While today ethologists are making extensive use of invasive techniques generally not available for research on humans (e.g., neuroanatomy), the classical methods of data collection in ethology are field observation with description of the behavior of animals in their natural habitat, and experimental manipulation of elements in this habitat. The motto of Tinbergen's article (1963, p. 412) was: "Contempt for simple observation is a lethal trait in any science." This holds by itself an important lesson for (c)cp: the relatively small number of observational studies in contemporary (c)cp has been deplored by seniors in the field (Jahoda, 2011).

4.1.1 Cause

"The study of causation is the study of preceding events which can be shown to contribute to the occurrence of the behavior" (Tinbergen, 1963, p. 418). Cause can be deterministic, implying that the behavior cannot but follow the initiating condition (think of reflexes and fixed action patterns; Manning & Dawkins 2012). "Cause" can also refer to conditions that increase the probability of a behavioral outcome, for example, when a given context enables or facilitates certain choices for action (Berry et al., 2011, refer to "antecedent-consequent relationships"). Most research in (c)cp is about causality in such a broader sense. An example demonstrating a highly probable cause is an analysis by Whiting (1994) showing that environmental temperature is related to baby-carrying practices. In warm climates, babies usually are carried in slings or shawls close to the mother's body; in cold regions, babies are positioned away from the body of the mother, in a cradle or on a carrying board. The likely causal variable is the extent of discomfort when the baby is wetting the mother, which is much higher in cold climates. The relationship is strong (a substantial proportion of the variance is explained), the postulated cause is plausible, and it is hard to think of confounding factors that would point to an alternative explanation. The search for causal relationships is the backbone of scientific analysis. Despite many errors that may have been committed (assuming there is merit to the earlier sections of this Element), the search for such relationships will remain central to research in (c)cp.

4.1.2 Function

The question of function is based on the axiom that a behavior pattern must be good for something; otherwise, it would not have evolved and been maintained through the phylogenetic history of a species up to the present time. Thus, Tinbergen's question of function amounts to asking how a behavior pattern contributes to the continued survival of a species (what is it good for?). For example, sticklebacks fan fresh water with their fins over the eggs in their nests. Experiments have shown that the eggs die if this does not happen, but they will hatch also when artificial means of ventilation are used (mentioned in Tinbergen, 1963). This example illustrates that the analysis of function follows the empirical cycle mentioned in Section 3. Initial observations are followed by tentative explanations and thereafter by experiments in which specific hypotheses are tested through manipulation of conditions.

Since Tinbergen (1963) formulated his questions, discussions on function have expanded greatly. One question is whether organisms or separate genes are to be seen as the unit of survival (Dawkins, 1976). In evolutionary psychology, Tooby and Cosmides (1990) formulated an adaptationist agenda, emphasizing that there has to be a direct genetic basis for any behavior adaptation. The key argument is that genes are required for transmission across generations. Not only social scientists have challenged strict genetic determinism (see Section 2.1.1); biologists have also done so, including students of evolution (Andrews et al., 2002). A famous notion is "spandrels" that are by-products of evolutionary adaptations rather than adaptive outcomes (Gould & Lewontin, 1979). A major example is the human brain that has enabled us to develop religion and technology, outcomes for which the brain cannot possibly have developed originally. Another important concept is "exaptations," features of behavior that now serve a specific function but originally evolved for some other function (Gould & Vrba, 1982). For example, feathers as found on birds are thought to have evolved initially for sexual display or temperature regulation and only later adapted to flight. The concepts of spandrels and exaptations and how they apply to behavior have led to extensive debates. One example is music, which is found in every human society. Did it evolve because it contributed to reproductive success (by impressing potential partners), to parent-infant bonding, or to social cohesion? Or is music to be seen as an exaptation or spandrel, an evolutionary byproduct of other skills (Honing et al., 2015). In summary, analyses by ethologists lead to all kinds of complexities, but they also point to perspectives that are complementary to those usually found in (c)cp.

The conceptual rationale for functionality expands when adaptations are not only seen as constraints but also as affordances that open up spaces of opportunities (Poortinga & Soudijn, 2002). In other words, a human group can adopt and maintain a certain behavior manifestation, as long as it is not detrimental to the long-term survival of the group. Ethologists tend to study the function of patterns of behavior that involve a sequence of distinguishable acts and the expression of several genes. Examples include attachment, courtship, ownership, prestige (honor), and sharing. Such patterns tend to be recognizable (i.e., observers agree on their identification) across a wide range of species, such as courtship displays that in form and function are easily identified in human adolescents and also in several species of birds.

The analysis of function can be highly problematic. Religious commitment is found in all human societies and often it is costly (demanding sacrifices, constraining desires, time to be spent on rituals, etc.). How can this make sense functionally? One argument is that religion is not an adaptation but has come about as a recurring by-product of some important adaptation (see Atran, 2007). Other authors have proposed more convergent theories, such as costly signaling theory (Zahavi & Zahavi, 1997). Leaving aside complexities (e.g., Maynard Smith & Harper, 2003), it can be said that costly physical traits, such as the proverbial tail of the peacock, signal high fitness. By extension, this principle can also pertain to costly behavior, including behavior displaying religious commitment. For example, using information from the United States in the nineteenth century, Sosis and Bresler (2003) found that communes that imposed costlier requirements survived for a longer time than did less demanding (often nonreligious) communes.

In a broad sweep, Norenzayan et al. (2014) have linked the emergence of moralistic (prosocial) religions to the emergence of complex societies with a greater need for mutual trust and cooperation. These authors argue that they provide a synthesis reconciling adaptationist approaches to religion with approaches that see religion as a mere by-product of evolution. However, interpretations of one-time developments in a distant past are difficult to examine critically. Ethologists at the time of Tinbergen would conduct meticulous empirical studies of function, collecting observational data. This standard of evidence is out of reach for complex and variable behavior patterns. At the same time, the loosening up of strict adaptationism and the introduction of recorded history, as noted in the study by Sosis and Bresler (2003), suggest that psychological function can be analyzed with more proximate data.

In summary, the apparent evidence for the function of manifest behavior can be striking (as with courtship displays) but also unclear (as with religion). Adaptations that are characteristic of a species can still differ in their manifestations, depending on environmental constraints. The study of function, even more than of Tinbergen's other three questions, involves theoretical argument (Cuthill, 2009). Empirically, functions need to be derived through identifying common themes underneath observable variations in manifest behavior. Especially in humans this is a complex task. The range of variation across contexts that c(c)p can contribute is important, if not indispensable, for advancing further understanding.

4.1.3 Phylogenetic Development of Behavior

When a distinction is made between proximate and ultimate explanation, phylogenetic development is about ultimate explanation, that is, the why and how of the emergence of behavior patterns in the course of evolution. In Darwinian theory, evolution is the change in heritable characteristics of biological populations over generations. The main mechanism of change is natural selection; slight variations in heritable individual characteristics lead to differences in rates of reproduction (differential fitness and adaptation). Other mechanisms, such as mutations, genetic drift, and selective migration can also play a role. Tinbergen (1963) saw two major aims for the study of evolution: clarification of the course of evolution and tracing how evolutionary changes came about. He also mentioned an evident difficulty, namely that behavior leaves few fossils. Another difficulty is that similarities, including similarities in function, do not necessarily reflect common origin. A distinction needs to be made between "homologies" (similarities due to shared ancestry) and "analogies" (independent evolution of similar features). A well-known example of an analogy are the eyes of the octopus and the human; there are remarkable structural and functional similarities, but no common origin.

Since Tinbergen (1963) formulated his questions, evolution theory has been further expanded. Some of these developments address cooperative behavior and are at the heart of social interactions in humans as well as other species. Hamilton (1964) introduced the principle of "inclusive fitness" that takes into consideration inheritance not only through direct offspring (the number of children a parent has) but also through relatives (with whom you share a large part of your genes). For humans, this may help explain why in all societies the most significant interpersonal relationships are among family members (e.g., Georgas et al., 2006). A second expansion of Darwinian theory is the concept of "reciprocal altruism" to explain cooperative behavior between genetically unrelated individuals (Trivers, 1971). Humans often display cooperative behavior even toward non-relatives. Theoretically, such behavior should occur only when there is an expectation that an actor's costs will be compensated for by future reciprocation. With economic games, cooperation has been demonstrated extensively, even under conditions where the more profitable strategy for an individual player is to maximize their own interest and become a "free rider" or "defector." Cooperative behavior is affected by a player's reputation; a less cooperative strategy tends to be chosen when a player in a game receives information about prior defection of another player (see, e.g., Fehr & Fischbacher, 2003; Hilbe et al., 2018). It may be noted that the validity of such explanations is in principle open to experimentation. A broad view has emerged in which cooperation is conceptualized as a necessary condition for all evolutionary change. In this view cooperation entails giving up reproductive potential to help others and this can be found through the entire tree of life, from single-cell organisms that combine to form multi-cell organisms, via eusocial insects, such as bees, to humans (Nowak, 2006).

The principle of evolution of behavior is the leading idea of evolutionary psychology. In empirical studies, regularities have been identified that appear to be present in all human societies and are deemed to be characteristic of our species. Well known are studies on mate selection (Buss, 1989; Walter et al., 2020). Men more than women have been found to prefer physically attractive mates younger than themselves and women have, more than men, a preference for older mates with good (financial) standing. The rationale is that men are attracted by signals in women of good health and the capacity to have children, while women are attracted by signals in men indicating the capacity of taking care of them and their children. An elaboration of such ideas is that mate selection processes can be the basis of further evolutionary development. For example, with data from forty-five countries, Conroy-Beam et al. (2019) have found that desirable traits converge to a cluster and lead to assortative mating patterns that in the long run may be expected to drive evolutionary change.

The role of the environmental context is elaborated further in the notion of the ecological niche, that is, how a species has evolved to live in and interact with its ecological environment (Laland et al., 2000, 2015). The emphasis is on how humans are active constructors of their environments – in other words, how they expand their range of affordances and how the resulting changes ultimately may even affect genetic evolutionary processes.

While in present-day biology, the two questions of function and phylogenetic development have much overlap, in psychology and (c)cp they may need to be considered separately, in so far as evolutionary pathways to current function are hard to reconstruct. At the time when Tinbergen (1963) formulated his four questions, the DNA machinery for genetic inheritance largely was still unknown. Although today anatomical and physiological features increasingly can be linked to genetic underpinnings and their history can be traced, evolutionary explanations of human behavior remain open to debate (e.g., Penn et al., 2008; Wynne & Bolhuis, 2009). Overall, an evolutionary perspective suggests that humans as a species are not so psychologically unique and populations within the species not so different as long believed.

4.1.4 Ontogenetic Development

The remaining question addresses "change of behavior machinery during development" (Tinbergen, 1963, p. 423). External influences controlling such changes are analyzed through manipulations of the environment; internal influences are inferred in the first instance from the ineffectiveness of such manipulations. According to Tinbergen, these interpretations need to be validated by direct interventions in internal (i.e., physiological) events in an organism. Evidently, for psychological research on humans, the latter route for validation is largely unavailable for ethical reasons. However, it is possible to compare developmental trajectories and outcomes with longitudinal and sometimes cross-sectional research designs across populations. As mentioned in Section 3, research contexts have the status of conditions in the sense of quasi-experiments. Thus, experimental designs can be used for the refutation of a postulated state of affairs. For example, Hewlett et al. (2012) report various findings on horizontal and oblique social learning (see Section 2.1.1) among hunter-gatherers in Central Africa that are incompatible with the viewpoint that social learning in such populations is largely from parents to children (vertical transmission).

Tinbergen explicitly relates ontogeny to function. From birth onward, an organism is equipped to participate in the ecologically and socially defined niche in which it is growing up; there is a complex set of relationships between genetic constitution and environment, and these relationships continue to change during the lifespan of an organism. While most research and thinking about ontogenetic development analyzes expansion of the behavior repertoire in the course of childhood and adolescence, "life-span psychology" also traces changes through adulthood and old age (Baltes, 1997; Baltes et al., 2006). In this line of thinking, the function of grandparents – and differences in this function between grandmothers and grandfathers – in bringing up children is part of an ontogenetic developmental perspective (Voland, Chasiotis, & Schiefenhövel, 2005).

Several research traditions in (c)cp with a developmental dimension address trajectories of development in cognition, language, motivation, autonomy, and so on across diverse contexts. In close-up, all kinds of differences have been observed across populations in developmental curves that map the level of achievement on some variable against age. From a broader perspective, similarities are striking: children are born with the potential to deal with demands of a wide range of contexts. Conditions in the external environment determine the content of the behavior repertoire that they will acquire. A telling illustration is the detailed observation of the behavior repertoire of a seven-year-old boy during one day in his life, reported by Barker and Wright (1951). The boy displays specific knowledge and competencies enabling him to deal successfully with a large variety of situations. Such impressive achievements are shown not only by this child but by children all over the world, each of them in their particular context. A point to note is the active participation of children in their own development. Especially Rogoff (e.g., 2014) has emphasized that children are "learning by observing and pitching in."

A complementary perspective reflects that much of a child's potential is *not* realized. Child (1954) defined socialization as the process through which individuals are led to develop actual behavior within a much narrower range than the potentialities they are born with. An illustration from psycholinguistics are the difficulties of learners of a new language with category boundaries that differ from their mother tongue; an iconic example is the difficulty Japanese speakers have in dealing with the "l" and the "r" in English (e.g., Goto, 1971). Apparently, distinctions between phonemic categories that are not used disappear in the course of development. Perhaps more striking is the vanishing of boundaries between conceptual categories that are available to young infants. The Korean language makes a distinction between two verbs denoting "tight fit" (*kkita*) and "loose fit" (*nehta*) for which there is no match in English. In habituation experiments, Hespos and Spelke (2004) found that five-month-old babies living in a monolingual English environment showed evidence of making this distinction long before the onset of speech. They concluded that some capacity must be involved that predates the human language faculty. This study is part of a broader discussion on the inheritance of perceptual and conceptual representations (e.g., Carey, 2008).

In a way, all theories of ontogenetic development attempt to answer Tinbergen's question. As is to be expected, such theories differ in emphasis. Earlier contrasts between theories based on "nature" (e.g., the maturational theory of Gesell, 1940) or "nurture" (e.g., the learning theory of Skinner, 1957) have largely dissipated; these two aspects are now generally seen as intertwined. Contemporary theories emphasize contextualism and a system orientation (Lerner, Levin-Bizan, & Warren, 2011), reflected in terms such as "bio-cultural" or "bio-eco-cultural" (e.g., Worthman, 2010). This implies that research has to extend beyond its predominantly Western database. Consideration of context adds a dimension of variation to the study of ontogenetic development. In the words of Heron and Kroeger (1981, p. 1): "Any serious attempt to study human behavior and experience must, in the very nature of things, be both developmental in depth and cross-cultural in breadth."

The context of the child has been formalized in various models. Bronfenbrenner (1979) described development as the outcome of the interaction between the individual and the surrounding context, represented as a set of nested structures consisting of the microsystem (the nuclear family), the mesosystem (neighborhood, school, etc.), and the macrosystem (societal goals and values). These various components are more or less open to direct observation and in empirical research mostly have the status of (proximal) causal variables. A somewhat similar frame was formulated by Super and Harkness (1986), called the "developmental niche," with three subsystems surrounding the child: (i) physical and social settings, (ii) customs and arrangements of childcare, and (iii) beliefs of caretakers about the nature of children. Effects of parental beliefs (called "parental ethnotheories" if deemed normative in a population) start at birth. Handling, beginning with newborns (Hopkins & Westra, 1990), shows early effects in the domain of psychomotor development, affecting the age at which babies are sitting up and start walking or crawling (e.g., Super, 1976).

An influential theory is Bowlby's (1969 attachment theory. Attachment behavior is conceived of as an evolutionary-based survival strategy to protect the young from predators. In part, the theory derives from findings in ethology, showing that young animals emit signals to which parents are predisposed to respond. The feeding behavior of birds provides persuasive illustrations, but humans also are equipped to react to signals, notably the crying of a baby, and somewhat later to smiling, reaching out, and other behaviors. Another root of Bowlby's theory is Freud's psychoanalysis with strong clinical overtones; Freud postulated early life stages as leading to encompassing and more or less fixed dispositions for the remainder of life. The combination of ethological and psychoanalytic elements is reflected in Bowlby's theory that insecure attachment, due to emotionally cold or absent primary caretakers, leads to negative consequences in adulthood. Further research by Belsky and others (e.g., Belsky, Steinberg, & Draper, 1991) has found support for such relationships; insecure attachment early in life is associated with early pubertal development and, in adulthood, unstable pair bonds and limited investment in child rearing. This creates conditions for repetition of the same pattern across generations. This work has expanded further to a search for a genetic basis and epigenetic pathways of development (e.g., Belsky, 2012). However, Cole and Cole (1996) concluded that the available evidence on the long-term consequences of various forms of attachment is mixed. Also Lamb and Lewis (2011) pointed out that the stability of attachment patterns over time may have to be explained in terms of continuity of parent-child interactions rather than as a characteristic of the child that has become settled early in life. In other words, if the Freudian perspective on attachment is left aside, developmental trajectories might be viewed as more flexible than construed by Bowlby. Part of the discussion is about warmth as a characteristic of care giving. Mesman et al. (2018) defend the notion that warmth is expressed universally; Keller et al. (2018) take the position that warmth is not a consistent aspect of care everywhere. The arguments tend to be reminiscent of the debate on the universality versus specificity of emotions (see Section 1.4). Part of the evidence mentioned by Keller et al. comes from societies where young children tend to be carried and sleep with the mother; could this perhaps make the need for other expressions of warmth less essential?

These brief comments show that the mission defined by Heron and Kroeger (1981) is not broad enough, if Tinbergen's (1963) questions are taken seriously. (C)cp should not only address variations in developmental trajectories across contexts but also consider the biological basis of human behavior (Hewlett & Lamb, 2002; Keller, Schölmerich, & Poortinga, 2002; Poortinga & Soudijn, 2002): "Humans are predisposed with a universal repertoire of developmental propensities that are emphasized or suppressed depending on environmental affordances and constraints" (Keller, 2019, p. 397). This quote summarizes why the analysis of ontogenetic development should be at the foundation of (c)cp as a field of research.

4.2 Changes in Behavior over Historical Time

At the time when Tinbergen suggested his four questions, ethologists mainly studied nonhuman species. Unsurprisingly, no question was formulated about changes in behavior patterns over the course of historical time (i.e., the period for which there is recorded history). However, a current behavior repertoire is likely to have roots in the past; humans are uniquely capable of passing accumulated knowledge, rituals, and skills across generations. Thus, for (c)cp, a fifth question is relevant in addition to Tinbergen's four: the question of the historical origin of a behavior pattern observed in a population.

As mentioned in Section 2.3, evident continuities in conventions can be traced back a long time. Some words denoting objects have undergone little change in meaning over millennia, and written symbols (e.g., letters) in scripts have remained recognizable over a similar period. In contrast, information about the origin and (dis)continuities in historical time of social behavior or ontogenetic development is harder to find and interpret. With a relatively short time perspective, in a data set with thirty countries, Georgas et al. (2006) found for many of these countries a similar shift in family relationships. The role of the father, traditionally the provider and authority figure, has been diminishing and the mother appears to have become even more the center of the nuclear family in contemporary societies. The likely reason for this change is lower dependence on the economic input of the father.

Studies of historical changes often take a broad sweep. For example, Kağıtçıbaşı (1997) reviews historical evidence of individualistic and collectivistic tendencies in various countries. For Europe, both kinds of tendencies are noted, suggesting variations among authors, countries, and behavior domains; however, such nuances disappear when in the end a dichotomy between East and West is upheld. In a historical analysis of the East-West distinction in cognition, Nisbett (2003; see Section 1.2) places the origin in ancient Greece and ancient China. For this account, the Middle Ages in Europe, when Greek traditions were hard to find, form a gap that appears to be at variance with historical continuity. Making even stronger claims, Ariès (1960) suggests on the basis of medieval European writings the absence of parental expressions of emotions with regard to children that are characteristic of contemporary families. He suggests that at the time, one's family and descent and arranged marriages were central rather than the romantic love relationship that forms the basis of partnerships today. It would appear that the account of Ariès is extremely doubtful, as it is incompatible with ethologically based insights about parental bonding and ontogenetic development.

Broad views about historical changes are found also with authors who see historicity as an essential characteristic of human psychological functioning. Most influential has been Vygotsky (1978), who postulated historical development for higher mental functions at the level of the society (see Section 1.2). Also in traditions of cultural psychology (Shweder, 1990) and sociocultural psychology (Valsiner, 2012; see Section 2.1), ideas and concepts are not primarily features of individuals, but they acquire existence (meaning) in historically situated interactions with others or with the society at large. An integrative view is held by Cole (1996; Cole & Packer, 2011. His approach was inspired by the Russian tradition of Vygotsky, with an important difference. As mentioned in Section 1.2, Cole emphasizes the principle of societal mediation and social-historical change in behavior over time at the level of specific skills and cognitive operations (which come close to conventions as mentioned in Section 2.3), rather than at the level of broad domains or functions. For Cole, historical time is part of a multilayered perspective on time, ranging from physical time and phylogenetic development via social-historical change and ontogenetic development to microgenesis (i.e., the here and now of human experience). Such views can be seen as complementary to Tinbergen's ideas.

4.3 Conclusion

Most research in (c)cp addresses differences in behavior from a single perspective, seeking a causal relation between some behavior outcome and some contextual antecedent. This section has argued for asking a broader range of questions. All five perspectives mentioned can hardly be addressed simultaneously in a single study, but the range of questions being considered needs to be informed by these various perspectives. This Element is not original in asking for integration and synthesis. For example, Liebal and Haun (2018) made a plea for a triadic approach including comparative (human-animal), developmental, and cross-cultural psychology, taking Tinbergen's four questions as a lead. A few decades ago, Hinde (1987) had already asked for the combination of evolutionary principles and approaches from ethology, psychology, and anthropology. If (c)cp is to play a significant role in the scientific debate, such integration seems inescapable.

5 Cross-Cultural and Cultural Psychology for the Global Village

This brief section asserts that for (c)cp as a field of knowledge, there is an important task at a time when nations and people worldwide are becoming more interconnected and interdependent, often expressed with the notion of the "global village." A reorientation is suggested with less emphasis on "culture" as a mediating factor and more emphasis on direct effects of external conditions on manifest behavior and well-being. The first subsection mentions economic poverty as a contextual condition with wide-ranging behavior correlates that distinguish the poor from the affluent. The second subsection identifies in applied (c)cp a trend toward contextual explanations in the balance between person and context, moving from essentializing to contextualizing population differences in behavior. The concluding subsection is a call for action in the face of increasing economic inequality, populism, and extremism.

5.1 Big and Important Differences

Economic affluence, more than any other factor, underlies differences in behavior between (i) countries, (ii) distinguishable populations within countries, and (iii) individuals within populations. Low affluence (poverty) denotes not only a lack of income; it entails "hunger and malnutrition, limited access to education and other basic services, social discrimination and exclusion, as well as the lack of participation in decision-making" (www.un.org/en/sections/issues-depth/poverty). Poverty amounts to a violation of human dignity and a denial of choices and opportunities (Sen, 1999). Ending poverty is the first of the seventeen Sustainable Development Goals (SDGs) of the 2030 Agenda for Sustainable Development (United Nations, 2017).

Affluence, expressed as GDP per capita or PPP (purchasing power parity), may be an economic variable, but it has strong psychological implications and correlates. Ratings of happiness (how much people enjoy their life) on a 10-point scale, obtained for samples in 162 countries since 2010, show means from as low as 3.4 in some African countries to as high as 8.3 for Scandinavian countries (Veenhoven, n.d.). These findings correspond with the World Happiness Report (Helliwell et al., 2020). This report is based on a broader perspective, including in addition to real GDP per capita five more variables: social support, healthy life expectancy, freedom to make life choices, generosity, and perceptions of corruption. Another indicator of the importance of affluence can be found in major values surveys where the first factor at the country level shows high correlation with GDP; for example, Hofstede (1980) found a correlation of $r = .82$ between the factor he labeled as individualism and GNP per capita.

Diener and colleagues (e.g., 2010) report a substantial positive relationship between income and well-being. Their extensive research program provides more insight into this relationship. The findings point to a distinction between two types of prosperity – economic and social psychological – and suggest that next to economic security, social security also matters for well-being and life satisfaction. A point to note is that beyond a certain level, more income does not lead to a further increase in happiness or satisfaction. However, for poor people this is irrelevant; their income does not nearly reach such a level.

Within societies, income inequality is related to a range of social issues. Poor health, low life expectancy, school drop out, and criminal activities are more common among those with low incomes (Wilkinson & Pickett, 2017). Despite the overall increase in wealth in many countries, inequalities in affluence have become larger rather than smaller over the past two centuries (Milanovic, 2009). From the literature, affluence emerges as the main dimension in a complex manifold of factors and relationships. Another dimension of this manifold is social inequality, as reflected in the Gini index, a measure of income inequality. Since the poor lack social power and influence (both across and within countries), the manifold extends to quality of life indices, such as trust and security, and to freedom and autonomy.

The effects of poverty and its continuation over generations led Lewis (1966) to formulate the notion of a "culture of poverty." This concept is open to criticism, because it tends to make poverty a characteristic of the poor rather than emphasizing the contextual impositions and limitations in social and cognitive functioning that come with poverty (e.g., Small et al., 2010). At the same time, poverty is pervasive, determining many aspects of the life of poor people and ultimately affecting their outlook and ambitions. One distressing example comes from a study by Singh and Tripathi (2010) who found that Indian villagers under long-term debt bondage (indentured labor contracts) were reluctant to be freed from their bondage; they feared the uncertainties that came with freedom. The example also illustrates that realizing changes in established behavior patterns may not be easy. To tease apart a complex of factors, sound methods of analysis are needed.

Although it may be difficult to bring about change, this can be done. There is not only documentation of immediate and long-term adverse effects of poverty and inequality but also how such effects can be ameliorated through intervention programs, especially for children (Barbarin & Richter, 2001; Grantham-McGregor et al. 2007; Pick & Sirkin, 2010). Optimal use of the methodological toolbox (see Section 3) should strengthen such programs and their outcomes.

5.2 Applied (C)cp and the Contextualization of Differences

For each area of application in psychology, there exist studies including more than one population; applied (c)cp covers a large field. A major theme in this Element has been to describe how findings tend to reflect prior conceptualizations of differences. In each area, there are studies that tend to "essentialize" differences in manifest behavior seeking explanations in terms of general dispositions, such as psychological traits, processes, and functions. Each area also has approaches that lean toward "contextualizing" differences. Areas with extensive coverage include acculturation and intergroup relations and the broad area of health (Berry et al., 2011).

In the area of health, an outstanding example of essential differences between populations can be found in culture-bound syndromes, referring to categories of mental illnesses found in some society and not elsewhere (e.g., Simons & Hughes, 1985). There is now a trend in psychiatry toward postulating universal diagnostic categories with a common core of symptoms, and local variations in reported complaints (e.g., Draguns & Tanaka-Matsumi, 2003). To address such local variations and to avoid stereotyping in diagnoses the Cultural Formulation Interview has been introduced in DSM-5 (the fifth edition of the *Diagnostic and Statistical Manual of Mental Disorders* of the American Psychiatric Association; www.psychiatry.org/). In the new version of the *International Classification of Diseases of the WHO* (ICD-11, see https://icd.who.int/en), traditional medicine is acknowledged, be it only as part of mainstream medicine. Psychiatrists and clinical therapists cannot ignore local "idioms of distress," that is, local modes of expressing suffering. For example, Hinton, Reis, and De Jong (2020) found among Cambodian refugees in a clinic that 54 percent had been bothered by ghost encounters during the previous month. The extent to which such experiences were reported showed a very high correlation ($r = .8$) with severity of PTSD (posttraumatic stress disorder). It may be noted that these authors integrate manifestations that are typical of local behavior repertoire and a presumably common diagnostic category; there is no apparent conflict between these two perspectives.

A somewhat similar trend can be found in the literature on acculturation (see also Section 2.2). In a well-known model of acculturation of migrants, Berry (1980) distinguished between four strategies (integration, assimilation, separation, and marginalization). These strategies were portrayed as characteristic of persons: migrants choose a strategy or perhaps a mixture of strategies. Bourhis et al. (1997) drew attention to the expectations that receiving societies have of migrants and the constraints that these impose on the acculturation preferences of migrants. Berry (2001) presented an expanded model that incorporated such modes of context as societal strategies (multiculturalism, melting pot, segregation, and exclusion). Evidently, this entails a shift from the person of the migrant to the context. The idea of acculturation as a more or less uniform process of change was challenged further; Arends-Tóth and Van de Vijver (2003) showed that the preferred acculturation strategy of migrants may differ across life domains, such as the private sphere and the public sphere.

In research on ethnocentrism there is also a tradition linking differences in outcomes directly to differences in prevailing conditions, without much reference to "culture" or some other intermediate variable. In a classical study, Brewer and Campbell (1976) examined mutual attitudes and stereotypes in thirty tribal societies in Africa. In a nutshell, they found that all groups rated themselves more positive than they were rated by other groups, while groups perceived as backward received less positive ratings than groups perceived as educated and affluent. More recent literature emphasizes that a positive view of one's own group need not imply a negative view of other groups; a positive sense of the in-group or positive social identity (see the next paragraph) need not imply a negative evaluation of others (Brewer, 2007; Verkuyten, 2014). Much research has been inspired by Allport's (1954) "contact hypothesis." This hypothesis specifies four factors that promote positive intergroup attitudes and interactions: (i) equal status between the groups in the interaction situation; (ii) common goals, including having a common enemy; (iii) actual cooperation between members of the groups; and (iv) sanctioning by an authority of the contact (think of parents who endorse cross-group friendships for their children). Pettigrew (2015; Pettigrew & Tropp, 2006) reviews the extensive empirical evidence on intergroup contacts across varied settings, age cohorts, and countries with more than one-quarter million participants. The overall conclusion is that exclusion and discrimination of others may be widespread in the human species, but that these processes are open to change. Allport's principles are eminently applicable; individually and as groups, we can practice exclusion and discrimination or we can promote intergroup contacts and social inclusion.

A psychological concept that covers both personhood and social context is identity; it is about how one views oneself both as a person and in relation to others. Adams and Van de Vijver (2017) present a nested model with three circles: personal identity at the core, relational identity as a second circle, and social identity at the outside. Personal identity covers experiences of self-continuity and self-coherence, as well as individual autonomy, needs, and values. Relational identity pertains to an individual's roles and the interactions with others. There is a personal aspect to this (e.g., how I perceive and act on my role as a father or as a professional), and there is a social aspect (the conventions, including legal rules, that pertain to these interactions). Social identity refers to membership of social groups, that is, the groups you belong to (in-groups) as distinct from groups of others (out-groups).

In (c)cp, much research on identity addresses issues of acculturation and intergroup relations (Berry et al., 2006; Ward, 2008). In these studies, identity development often is associated with constraints. For example, the strong marginalization of the Roma, the largest indigenous minority in Europe, appears to have major implications not only for their social identity but also for their personal and relational identity (Dimitrova et al., 2014). In contrast, an open society offers a space of affordances for identity development. The mere categorization of people into two groups (e.g., when playing sports) is sufficient to create a sense of group membership – the well-known "minimal group paradigm" (Tajfel & Turner, 1979). In the emerging "superdiverse" urban societies (see Section 2.2), most people belong to multiple groups varying in composition over time and situations. There should be no lack of opportunity for development, including identity development; the question is whether societies in the global village can move to more openness. The question for (c) cp is how its conceptual and methodological tools can be mobilized for this purpose.

5.3 Threats to the Village, a Call for Action

In the decades after the Second World War, various regions of the world experienced periods of rapid economic growth. There was a sense of optimism that the world could become a better place for all, in terms of well-being as well as economic development. Eradication of poverty through education and economic growth and eradication of discrimination and human rights violations were was portrayed as a realistic goal. Warnings about high population growth, limits to the potential for economic expansion – raised by the Club of Rome in 1972 – and, particularly, serious effects of human activity on the world's climate mostly were ignored. Pessimism is now replacing optimism at a global scale. Youngsters, especially, are becoming concerned about the consequences of climate change and environmental pollution. Reduction of poverty is exceedingly slow; in several countries, the income of the majority of the population continues to be less $1.90 per day, the extreme poverty line (World Bank data; www.worldbank.org). In several low-income countries, the percentage of population growth is still higher than the growth in GNP. The traditional model of developmental economics that entailed great promises for low-income countries but was advantageous mainly to affluent countries as the costs of raw materials were kept low has lost credibility (Easterly, 2006).

At the same time, almost unbridled capitalism continues to be the main economic model across and within many countries. A report by Oxfam (2015) estimated that more than half of the world's economic assets are owned by less than 1 percent of the world's population. Even in 2020 when COVID-19 wrecked economies, the super rich became wealthier. A significant economic analysis challenging the current capitalist order by the French economist Piketty (2014) concludes that growing wealth and income inequality is inherent to capitalism and can only be reversed though state intervention. Unless this happens – Piketty proposes a global tax on wealth – the democratic order is threatened.

Is this not what we see happening in the global village right now? Inequality is at the heart of a poisonous mixture of discontent, discrimination, populism, and extremism. This mixture is the food stock for anti-democratic political movements that are exploited by Machiavellian leaders. As such, inequality is a threat to democratic processes of government and ultimately to the human rights of citizens. *Extremism* refers to any political or religious ideology about which there is consensus among those who do not subscribe to it that it is beyond the acceptable. Research on mechanisms promoting extremism has found that insecurity and uncertainty can motivate people to identify with groups that provide a distinctive identity (Hogg, 2014). This provides a link to *populism*, the core of which is an antagonism between the people and some elite (Panizza, 2005), with strong overtones of "good" and "evil." Populism centers on manipulation of opinions and attitudes, with often counterintuitive outcomes. How can voters in numerous countries fall on a large scale for the lure of capitalist parties known to advance the interests of a wealthy elite? Again, there remains work to do, identifying the psychological factors at play and exposing them.

As scientists and professionals, we like to see ourselves as an elite in society. The basis for this claim is that we have expert knowledge and skills. Perhaps we should go a step further and consider ourselves to be an elite not only by virtue of our knowledge base but also because our arguments, in so far as they are based on reason and empirical evidence, should lead to more balanced viewpoints than those of Machiavellian politicians and self-serving capitalists. If so, our responsibilities are even greater. While governments react to extremism with hard power, behavioral and social scientists will use soft power; education and intervention programs in the long run are probably more effective and certainly less destructive than weapons. In the global village, we have to interact with our neighbors; we have common interests that are threatened by economic inequality and presumed contrasts between us and others, nurtured by extremism and populism. If c(c)p changes its focus, it is well placed to emphasize the psychological unity of the village community underneath all the observable differences.

6 Epilogue

Research in cultural and cross-cultural psychology, (c)cp, has made much progress in mapping behavior differences between human populations. This Element discusses the general orientation of the field and finds that its history is characterized by emphasis on psychological differences between populations rather than how much humans are alike psychologically. A worrisome question that was raised is whether this orientation may facilitate stereotyping. It is suggested that the core concept of "culture" is too vague to guide critical analysis and interpretation of data. Probably this concept should be avoided for research in (c)cp, akin to the disappearance of the concept of "soul" or "psyche" from research in psychology.

Methodological and psychometric tools are outlined that allow carefully designed studies, with attention to identification of possible bias in data and examination of the replicability of findings. Such studies require large research teams with equitable input from team members representative of the entire range of populations involved, in all stages of a study and not just for data collection. To advance basic research, multiple questions will have to be asked simultaneously about the cause, the function, the deep and recent history, and the ontogenetic development of behavior patterns.

In the meantime, the global village is facing continuing poverty and inequality, as well as rising populism and extremism. Psychologists accustomed to looking beyond the boundaries of their own context have the urgent task to deploy their expertise for advancing individual well-being and community building in the village.

References

Adair, J., & Diaz-Loving, R. (1999). Indigenous psychologies: The meaning of the concept and its assessment. *Applied Psychology, 48*, 397–402.

Adams, B. G., & van de Vijver, F. J. R. (2017). Identity and acculturation: The case for Africa. *Journal of Psychology in Africa, 27*, 115–121.

Allport, G. W. (1954). *The nature of prejudice*. Reading, MA: Addison-Wesley.

American Psychiatric Association. (2013, May 3). Release Number 13–33.

Andrews, P. W., Gangestad, S. W., & Matthews, D. (2002). Adaptationism – how to carry out an exaptationist program. *Behavioral and Brain Sciences, 25*, 489–553.

Aplin, L. M., Farine, D. R., Morand-Ferron, J., Cockburn, A., Thornton, A., & Sheldon, B. C. (2015). Experimentally induced innovations lead to persistent culture via conformity in wild birds. *Nature, 518*, 538–541.

Arends-Tóth, J., & van de Vijver, F. (2003). Multiculturalism and acculturation: Views of Dutch and Turkish-Dutch. *European Journal of Social Psychology, 33*, 249–266.

Ariès, P. (1960). *L'enfant et la vie familiale sous l'Ancien Régime* [Child and family life in the Old Order]. Paris: Éditions du Seuil.

Atran, S. (2007). Religion's social and cognitive landscape. In S. Kitayama & D. Cohen (Eds.), *Handbook of cultural psychology* (pp. 437–453). New York: Guildford Press.

Baldwin, J. R., Faulkner, S. L., & Hecht, M. L. (2006). A moving target: The illusive definition of culture. In J. R. Baldwin, S. L. Faulkner, M. L. Hecht, & S. L. Lindsley (Eds.), *Redefining culture: Perspectives across the disciplines* (pp. 3–26). Mahwah, NJ: Erlbaum.

Baltes, P. B. (1997). On the incomplete architecture of human ontogeny. *American Psychologist, 52*, 366–380.

Baltes, P. B., Reuter-Lorenz, P. A., & Rösler, F. (Eds.). (2006). *Lifespan development and the brain: The perspective of biocultural co-constructivism*. Cambridge: Cambridge University Press.

Bandura, A. (1977). *Social learning theory*. Englewood Cliffs, NJ: Prentice Hall.

Barbarin, O. A., & Richter, L. M. (2001). *Mandela's children: Growing up in post-apartheid South Africa*. London: Routledge.

Barker, R. G., & Wright, L. S. (1951). *One boy's day: A specimen record of behavior*. New York: Harper.

Barrett, L. F., Adolphs, R., Marsella, S., Martinez, A. M., & Pollak, S. D. (2019). Emotional expressions reconsidered: Challenges to inferring emotion from human facial movements. *Psychological Science in the Public Interest*, *20*(1), 1–68.

Bebko, G. M., Cheon, B. K., Ochsner, K. N., & Chiao, J. Y. (2019). Cultural differences in perceptual strategies underlying emotion. *Journal of Cross-Cultural Psychology*, *50*, 1014–1026.

Belsky, J. (2012). The development of human reproductive strategies: Progress and prospects. *Current Directions in Psychological Science*, *21*(5), 310–316.

Belsky, J., Steinberg, L., & Draper, P. (1991). Childhood experience, interpersonal development, and reproductive strategy: An evolutionary theory of socialization. *Child Development*, *62*, 647–670.

Bender, M., & Adams B. G. (Eds.). (2021). *Methods and assessment in culture and psychology*. Cambridge: Cambridge University Press.

Benítez, I., Padilla, J. L., van de Vijver, F., & Cuevas, A. (2018). What cognitive interviews tell us about bias in cross-cultural research: An illustration using quality-of-life items. *Field Methods*, *30*(4), 277–294.

Berlin, B., & Kay, P. (1969). *Basic color terms: Their universality and evolution*. Berkeley: University of California Press.

Bernardi, J., & Jobson, L. (2019). Investigating the moderating role of culture on the relationship between appraisals and symptoms of posttraumatic stress disorder. *Clinical Psychological Science*, *7*, 1000–1013.

Berry, J. W. (1980). Acculturation as varieties of adaptation. In A. Padilla (Ed.), *Acculturation: Theory, models and some new findings* (pp. 9–25). Boulder, CO: Westview.

Berry, J. W. (1997). Immigration, acculturation and adaptation. *Applied Psychology: An International Review*, *46*, 5–68.

Berry, J. W. (2001). A psychology of immigration. *Journal of Social Issues*, *57*, 615–631.

Berry, J. W., Phinney, J. S., Sam, D. L., & Vedder, P. (Eds.). (2006). *Immigrant youth in cultural transition: Acculturation, identity, and adaptation across national contexts*. Mahwah, NJ: Erlbaum.

Berry, J. W., Poortinga, Y. H., Breugelmans, S. M., Chasiotis, A., & Sam, D. L. (2011). *Cross-cultural psychology: Research and applications* (3rd ed.). Cambridge: Cambridge University Press.

Bimler, D. (2007). From color naming to a language space: An analysis of data from the World Color Survey. *Journal of Cognition and Culture*, *7*, 173–199.

Birdwhistell, R. L. (1970). *Kinesics and context*. Philadelphia: University of Pennsylvania Press.

Boehnke, K., Lietz, P., Schreier, M., & Wilhelm, A. (2011). Sampling: The selection of cases for culturally comparative psychological research. In

D. Matsumoto & F. J. R. Van de Vijver (Eds.), *Cross-cultural research methods in psychology* (pp. 102–129). New York: Cambridge University Press.

Boer, D., Hanke, K., & He, J. (2018). On detecting systematic measurement error in cross-cultural research: A review and critical reflection on equivalence and invariance tests. *Journal of Cross-Cultural Psychology, 49,* 713–734.

Bolhuis, J. J., & Verhulst, S. (2009). *Tinbergen's legacy: Function and mechanism in behavioral biology.* Cambridge: Cambridge University Press.

Bolhuis, J. J., & Wynne, C. D. L. (2009). Can evolution explain how minds work? *Nature, 458,* 832–833.

Boroditsky, L., Schmidt, L. A., & Phillips, W. (2003). In D. Gentner & S. Goldin-Meadow (Eds.), *Language in mind: Advances in the study of language and thought* (pp. 61–79). Cambridge, MA: MIT Press.

Botvinik-Nezer, R., Holzmeister, F., Camerer, C. F., Dreber, A., Huber, J. Johannesson, M. ... Scholnberg, T. (2020). Variability in the analysis of a single neuroimaging dataset by many teams. *Nature, 582,* 84–88.

Bourhis, R., Moise, C., Perreault, S., & Senecal, S. (1997). Towards an interactive acculturation model: A social psychological approach. *International Journal of Psychology, 32,* 369–386.

Bowlby, J. (1969). *Attachment and loss.* Vol. I: *Attachment.* New York: Basic Books.

Boyd, R., & Richerson, P. J. (1985). *Culture and the evolutionary process.* Chicago: University of Chicago Press.

Breugelmans, S. M., & Poortinga, Y. H. (2006). Emotion without a word: Shame and guilt with Rarámuri Indians and rural Javanese. *Journal of Personality and Social Psychology, 91,* 1111–1122.

Brewer, M. B. (2007). The importance of being *we:* Human nature and intergroup relations. *American Psychologist, 62,* 728–738.

Brewer, M., & Campbell, D. T. (1976). *Ethnocentrism and intergroup attitudes: East African evidence.* London: Sage.

Bronfenbrenner, U. (1979). *The ecology of human development.* Cambridge, MA: Harvard University Press.

Brouwers, S. A., Van Hemert, D. A., Breugelmans, S. M., & van de Vijver, F. J. R. (2004). A historical analysis of empirical studies published in the *Journal of Cross-Cultural Psychology* 1970–2004. *Journal of Cross-Cultural Psychology, 35,* 251–262.

Bruner, J. (1990). *Acts of meaning.* Cambridge, MA: Harvard University Press.

Bryman, A. (2015). *Social research methods* (5th ed.) Oxford: Oxford University Press.

Buss, D. M. (1989). Sex differences in human mate preferences: Evolutionary hypotheses tested in 37 cultures. *Behavioral and Brain Sciences, 12,* 1–14.

Button, K. S., Ioannidis, J. P. A., Mokrysz, C., Nosek, J. F., Robinson, E. S. J., & Munafò, M. R. Nosek, J. . (2013). Power failure: Why small sample size undermines the reliability of neuroscience. *Nature Reviews Neuroscience, 14,* 365–376.

Byrne, B. M., & Van de Vijver, F. J. R. (2010). Testing for measurement and structural equivalence in large-scale cross-cultural studies: Addressing the issue of nonequivalence. *International Journal of Testing, 10,* 107–132.

Campbell, D. T. (1964). Distinguishing differences of perception from failures of communication in cross-cultural studies. In F. S. C. Northrop & H. H. Livingston (Eds.), *Cross-cultural understanding: Epistemology in anthropology* (pp. 308–336). New York: Harper & Row.

Campbell, D. T., & Fiske, D. W. (1959). Convergent and discriminant validation by the multitrait-multimethod matrix. *Psychological Bulletin, 56,* 81–105.

Carey, S. (2008). Précis of *The origin of concepts. Behavioral and Brain Sciences, 34,* 113–167.

Cavalli-Sforza, L. L., & Feldman, M. (1981). *Cultural transmission and evolution: A quantitative approach.* Princeton, NJ: Princeton University Press.

Chen, C., & Moyzis, R. K. (2018). Cultural genomics: Promises and challenges. *Journal of Cross-Cultural Psychology, 49,* 764–788.

Cheung, F. M., Leung, K., Fan, R. M., Song, W., Zhang, J., & Zhang, J. (1996). Development of the Chinese Personality Assessment Inventory. *Journal of Cross-Cultural Psychology, 27,* 181–199.

Cheung, S. F., Cheung, F. M., Howard, R., & Lin, Y.-H. (2006). Personality across the ethnic divide in Singapore: Are "Chinese traits" uniquely Chinese? *Personality and Individual Differences, 41,* 467–477.

Chiao, J. Y., Harada, T., Komeda, H., Li, A., Mano, Y., Saito, D. . . . Iidaka, T. (2009). Neural basis of individualistic and collectivistic views of self. *Human Brain Mapping, 30,* 2813–2820.

Child, I. L. (1954). Socialization. In G. Lindzey (Ed.), *Handbook of social psychology* (Vol. 2, pp. 655–692). Cambridge, MA: Addison-Wesley.

Church, A. T. (2016). Personality traits across cultures. *Current Opinion in Psychology, 8,* 22–30.

Cohen D., & Kitayama, S. (Eds.) (2019). *Handbook of cultural psychology* (2nd ed.). New York: Guildford Press.

Cohen, J. (1994). The earth is round (*p* < .05). *American Psychologist, 49,* 997–1003.

Cole, M. (1996). *Cultural psychology: A once and future discipline.* Cambridge, MA: Harvard University Press.

Cole, M., & Cole, S. R. (1996). *The development of children* (3rd ed.). New York Freeman.

Cole, M., Gay, J., Glick, J., & Sharp, D. (1971). *The cultural context of learning and thinking*. New York: Basic Books.

Cole, M., & Packer, M. (2011). Culture in development. In M. E. Lamb & M. H. Bornstein (Eds.), *Social and personality development: An advanced textbook* (6th ed., pp. 51–108). New York: Psychology Press.

Conroy-Beam, D., Roneya, J. R., Lukaszewski, A. W., Buss, D. M., Asao, K., Sorokowska, A. Zupančič, M. (2019). Assortative mating and the evolution of desirability covariation. *Evolution and Human Behavior, 40*, 479–491.

Corbin, J. M., & Strauss, A. (1990). Grounded theory research: Procedures, canons, and evaluative criteria. *Qualitative Sociology, 13*(1), 3–21.

Creswell, J. W. (2009). *Research design: Qualitative, quantitative, and mixed methods approaches* (3rd ed.). Los Angeles: Sage.

Cronbach, L. J., Gleser, G. C., Nanda, H., & Rajaratnam, N. (1972). *The dependability of behavioral measurements*. New York: Wiley.

Cuthill, I. (2009). The study of function in behavioral ecology. In J. J. Bolhuis & S. Verhulst (Eds.) (2009). *Tinbergen's legacy: Function and mechanism in behavioral biology* (pp. 107–126). Cambridge: Cambridge University Press.

Dasen, P. R. (1972). Cross-cultural Piagetian research: A summary. *Journal of Cross-Cultural Psychology, 7*, 75–85.

Dasen, P. R. (1984). The cross-cultural study of intelligence: Piaget and the Baoulé. *International Journal of Psychology, 19*, 407–434.

Dasen, P. R., & Mishra, R. C. (2010). *Development of geocentric spatial language and cognition*. Cambridge: Cambridge University Press.

Dawkins, R. (1976). *The selfish gene*. New York: Oxford University Press.

de Groot, A. D., & Spiekerman J. A. A. (1969). *Methodologies: Foundations of inference and research in the behavioral sciences*. The Hague: De Gruyter Mouton.

de Waal, F. B. M. (2008). Putting the altruism back into altruism: The evolution of empathy. *Annual Review of Psychology, 59*, 279–300.

Deręgowski, J. B. (1980). *Illusions, patterns and pictures: A cross-cultural perspective*. London: Academic Press.

Deręgowski, J. B. (1989). Real space and represented space: Cross-cultural perspectives. *Behavioral and Brain Sciences, 12*, 51–74.

Diaz-Guerrero, R. (1975). *Psychology of the Mexican: Culture and personality*. Austin: University of Texas Press.

Diener, F., Ng, W., Harter, J., & Arora, R. (2010). Wealth and happiness across the world: Material prosperity predicts life evaluation, whereas psychosocial prosperity predicts positive feeling. *Journal of Personality and Social Psychology, 99*, 52–61.

Diener, E., Oishi, S., & Lucas, R. E. (2015). National accounts of subjective well-being. *American Psychologist, 70*, 234–242.

Dimitrova, R., Chasiotis, A., Bender, M., & Van de Vijver, F. J. R. (2014). Collective identity and well-being of Bulgarian Roma adolescents and their mothers. *Journal of Youth and Adolescence, 43*, 375–386.

Doan, S. N., & Wang, Q. (2018). Children's emotion knowledge and internalizing problems: The moderating role of culture. *Transcultural Psychiatry, 55*, 689–709.

Doyen, S., Klein, O., Pichon, C.-L., & Cleeremans, A. (2012). Behavioral priming: It's all in the mind, but whose mind? *PLoS ONE, 7* (1), ArtID: e29081.

Draguns, J. G., & Tanaka-Matsumi, J. (2003). Assessment of psychopathology across and within cultures: Issues and findings. *Behaviour Research and Therapy, 41*, 755–775.

Easterly, W. (2006). *The white man's burden: Why the West's efforts to aid the rest have done so much ill and so little good.* Oxford: Oxford University Press.

Ekman, P., & Friesen, W. V. (1971). Constants across cultures in the face and emotion. *Journal of Personality and Social Psychology, 17*, 124–129.

Elfenbein, H. A. (2013). Nonverbal dialects and accents in facial expressions of emotion. *Emotion Review, 5*, 90–96.

Elfenbein, H. A., & Ambady, N. (2002). On the universality and cultural specificity of emotion recognition: A metaanalysis. *Psychological Bulletin, 128*, 203–235.

Ellemers, N., Fiske, S. T., Abele, A. E., Koch, A., & Yzerbyt, V. (2020). Adversarial alignment enables competing models to engage in cooperative theory building toward cumulative science. *PNAS, 117*(14), 7561–7567.

Evans, K., Rotello C. M., Li, X. S., & Rayner, K. (2009). Scene perception and memory revealed by eye movements and receiver-operating characteristic analyses: Does a cultural difference truly exist? *The Quarterly Journal of Experimental Psychology, 62*, 276–285.

Fehr, E., & Fischbacher, U. (2003). The nature of human altruism. *Nature, 425*, 785–791.

Fischer, R. (2018). *Personality, values, culture: An evolutionary approach.* Cambridge: Cambridge University Press.

Fischer, R. (2020). *People overestimate cultural differences in human values: The paradox of essentializing culture.* Manuscript in preparation.

Fischer, R., & Poortinga, Y. H. (2012). Are cultural values the same as the values of individuals? An examination of similarities in personal, social and cultural value structure. *International Journal of Cross-Cultural Management, 12*, 157–170.

Fischer, R., & Schwartz, S. H. (2011). Whence differences in value priorities? Individual, cultural, or artifactual sources. *Journal of Cross-Cultural Psychology, 42*, 1127–1144.

Fischer, R., Vauclair, C. M., Fontaine, J. J. R., & Schwartz, S. H. (2010). Are individual-level and country-level value structures different? Testing Hofstede's legacy with the Schwartz Value Survey. *Journal of Cross-Cultural Psychology, 41*, 135–151.

Fontaine, J. (2005). Equivalence. In K. Kempf-Leonard (Ed.), *Encyclopedia of social measurement* (Vol. 1, pp. 803–813). New York: Academic Press.

Fontaine, J. R. J., & Veirman, E., & Groenvynck, H. (2013). The dimensional structure of emotional experiences. In J. J. R. Fontaine, K. R. Scherer, & C. Soriano (Eds.), *Components of emotional meaning: A sourcebook* (pp. 233–242). Oxford: Oxford University Press.

Fortin Morales, A. M., Van de Vijver, F. J. R., & Poortinga, Y. H. (2013). Differential item functioning and educational risk factors in Guatemalan reading assessment. *Revista Interamericana de Psicología, 47*, 423–432.

Fuentes, A. (2006). Evolution is important but it is not simple: Defining cultural traits and incorporating complex evolutionary theory. *Behavioral and Brain Sciences, 29*, 354–355.

Geertz, C. (1973). *The interpretation of cultures*. New York: Basic Books.

Gelfand, M. J., Raver, J. L., Nishii, L., Leslie, L. M., Lun, J., Lim, B. C. … Yamaguchi, S. (2011). Differences between tight and loose cultures: A 33-nation study. *Science, 332*, 1100–1104.

Georgas, J., Berry, J. W., Van de Vijver, F., Kağıtçıbaşı, Ç. , & Poortinga, Y. (Eds.) (2006). *Families across cultures: A 30-nation psychological study*. Cambridge: Cambridge University Press.

Gergen, K. J. (1985). The social constructionist movement in modern psychology. *American Psychologist, 40*, 266–275.

Gesell, A. (1940). *The first five years of life: A guide to the study of the preschool child* (Part I). New York: Harper.

Girndt, T., & Poortinga, Y. H. (1997). Interculturele communicatie: Conventies en misverstanden. [Intercultural communication: Conventions and misunderstandings] *De Psycholoog, 32*, 299–304.

Goodall, J. (1986). *The chimpanzees of Gombe: Patterns of behavior*. Boston: Belknap.

Goto, H. (1971). Auditory perception by normal Japanese adults of sounds of "l" or "r." *Neuropsychologia, 9*, 317–323.

Gould, S. J., & Lewontin, R. C. (1979). The spandrels of San Marco and the Panglossian paradigm: A critique of the adaptationist programme. *Proceedings of the Royal Society of London* (Series B), *205*, 581–598.

Gould, S. J., & Vrba, E. S. (1982). Exaptation: A missing term in the science of form. *Paleobiology, 8*, 4–15.

Grantham-McGregor S., Cheung, Y. B., Cueto, S., Glewwe, P., Richter, L. Strupp, B. & International Child Development Steering Group. (2007). Developmental potential in the first 5 years for children in developing countries. *Lancet, 369*, 60–70.

Gross, P. R., Levitt, N., & Lewis, M. W. (Eds.) (1996). *The flight from science and reason.* Annals of the New York Academy of Sciences, Vol. 775. New York: New York Academy of Sciences.

Guba, E. G. (1981). Criteria for assessing the trustworthiness of naturalistic inquiries. *Educational Communication and Technology Journal, 29*, 75–91.

Hamilton, W. D. (1964). The genetical evolution of social behavior, I, II. *Journal of Theoretical Biology, 7*, 1–52.

Han, S. H., & Northoff, G. (2008). Culture-sensitive neural substrates of human cognition: A transcultural neuroimaging approach. *Nature Reviews Neuroscience, 9*, 646–654.

Hao, J., Li, D., Peng, L., Peng, S., & Torelli, C. J. (2016). Advancing our understanding of culture mixing. *Journal of Cross-Cultural Psychology, 47*, 1257–1267.

Haven, T. L., & Van Grootel, L. (2019). Preregistering qualitative research. *Accountability in Research, 26*, 229–244.

He, J., & Van de Vijver, F. J. R., , Espinosa Domínguez, A., & Mui, P. H. C. (2014). Toward a unification of acquiescent, extreme, and midpoint response styles: A multilevel study. *International Journal of Cross Cultural Management, 14*, 306–322.

Hedden, T., Ketay, S., Aron, A., Markus, H. R., & Gabriel, J. D. E. (2008). Cultural influences on neural substrates of attentional control. *Psychological Science, 19*, 12–17.

Heine, S. J., Lehman, D. R., Peng, K. P., & Greenholtz, J. (2002). What's wrong with cross-cultural comparisons of subjective Likert scales? The reference-group effect. *Journal of Personality and Social Psychology, 82*, 903–918.

Helliwell, J. F., Layard, R., Sachs, J., & De Neve J.-E. (Eds.). (2020). *World Happiness Report 2020.* New York: Sustainable Development Solutions Network.

Heron, A., & Kroeger, E. (1981). Introduction to developmental psychology. In H. C. Triandis & A. Heron (Eds.), *Handbook of cross-cultural psychology* (Vol. 4, pp. 1–15). Boston: Allyn & Bacon.

Hespos, S. J., & Spelke, E. S. (2004). Conceptual precursors to language. *Nature, 430*, 453–456.

Hewlett, B. S., Fouts, H. N., Boyette, A. H., & Hewlett, B. L. (2012). Social learning among Congo Basin hunter-gatherers. In A. Whiten, R. A., Hinde, C. B. Stringer, & K. N. Laland, (Eds.), *Culture evolves* (pp. 411–430). Oxford: Oxford University Press.

Hewlett, B. S., & Lamb, M. E. (2002). Integrating evolution, culture and developmental psychology: Explaining caregiver-infant proximity and responsiveness in central Africa and the USA. In H. Keller, Y. H. Poortinga, & A. Schölmerich (Eds.). (2002). *Between culture and biology: Perspectives on ontogenetic development.* (pp. 241–269). Cambridge: Cambridge University Press.

Hilbe, C., Schmid, L., Tkadlec, J., Chatterjee, K., & Nowak, M. A. (2018). Indirect reciprocity with private, noisy, and incomplete information. *PNAS, 115*(48), 12241–12246.

Hinde, R. A. (1987). *Individuals, relationships, and culture: Links between ethology and the social sciences.* Cambridge: Cambridge University Press.

Hinton, D. E., Reis, R., & de Jong, J. (2020). Ghost encounters among traumatized Cambodian refugees: Severity, relationship to PTSD, and phenomenology. *Culture, Medicine, and Psychiatry, 44*(3), 333–359.

Hofstede, G. (1980). *Culture's consequences: International differences in work-related values.* Beverly Hills, CA: Sage.

Hogg, M. A. (2014). From uncertainty to extremism: Social categorization and identity processes. *Current Directions in Psychological Science, 23*, 338–342.

Hong, Y., Morris, M., Chiu, C., & Benet-Martínez, V. (2000). Multicultural minds: A dynamic constructivist approach to culture and cognition. *American Psychologist, 55*, 709–720.

Honing, H., ten Cate, C., Peretz, I., & Trehub, S. E. (2015). Without it no music: Cognition, biology and evolution of musicality. *Philosophical Transactions of the Royal Society (Series B)* 370: 2014.0088.

Hopkins, B., & Westra, T. (1990). Motor development, maternal expectations, and the role of handling. *Infant Behavior and Development, 13*, 117–122.

Hox, J. (2010). *Multilevel analysis: Techniques and applications* (2nd ed.). London: Routledge.

Huang, Y., Tse, C. S., & Cho, K. W. (2014). Living in the North is not necessarily favorable: Different metaphoric associations between cardinal direction and valence in Hong Kong and in the United States. *European Journal of Social Psychology, 44*, 360–369.

Iacoboni, M. (2009). Imitation, empathy, and mirror neurons. *Annual Review of Psychology, 60*, 653–670.

Ioannidis, J. P. A. (2005). Why most published research findings are false. *PLoS Medicine 2*(8), e124.

Jahoda, G. (1992). *Crossroads between culture and mind.* New York: Harvester Wheatsheaf.

Jahoda, G. (2011). Past and present of cross-cultural psychology. In F. J. R. Van de Vijver, A. Chasiotis, & S. M. Breugelmans (Eds.), *Fundamental questions in cross-cultural psychology* (pp. 37–63). Cambridge, Cambridge University Press.

Jahoda, G. (2012). Critical reflections on some recent definitions of "culture." *Culture & Psychology, 18*(3), 289–303.

Jahoda, G., & Krewer, B. (1997). History of cross-cultural and cultural psychology. In J. W. Berry, Y. H. Poortinga, & J. Pandey (Eds.), *Handbook of cross-cultural psychology: Theory and method* (2nd ed., Vol. 1, pp. 1–42). Boston: Allyn & Bacon.

Kağıtçıbaşı, C. (1997). Individualism and collectivism. In J. W. Berry, M. H. Segall, & Ç. Kağıtçıbaşı (Eds.), *Handbook of cross-cultural psychology* (2nd ed., Vol 3, pp. 1–49). Boston: Allyn & Bacon.

Karasz, A. (2011). Qualitative and mixed methods research in cross-cultural psychology. In F. J. R. Van de Vijver, A. Chasiotis, & S. M. Breugelmans (Eds.), *Fundamental questions in cross-cultural psychology* (pp. 214–234). Cambridge: Cambridge University Press.

Kashima, Y., & Gelfand, M. J. (2012). A history of culture in psychology. In A. W. Kruglanski & W. Stroebe (Eds.), *Handbook of the history of social psychology* (pp. 499–520). New York: Psychology Press.

Kay, P., Berlin, B., Maffi, L., Merrifield, W. R., & Cook, R. (2009). *The World Color Survey.* Stanford, CA: CSLI Publications.

Keller, H. (2002). Development as the interface between biology and culture: A conceptualization of early ontogenetic experiences. In H. Keller, Y. Poortinga, & A. Schoelmerich (Eds.), *Between culture and biology* (pp. 215–240). Cambridge: Cambridge University Press.

Keller, H. (2019). Culture and development. In S. Kitayama & D. Cohen (Eds.), *Handbook of cultural psychology* (2nd ed., pp. 397–423). New York: Guildford Press.

Keller, H., Bard, K., Morelli, G. Chaudhary, N., Vicedo, M., Rosabal-Coto, M. ... Gottlieb, A. (2018). The myth of universal sensitive responsiveness: Comment on Mesman et al. (2017). *Child Development, 89*, 1921–1928.

Keller, H., Poortinga, Y. H., & Schoelmerich, A. (Eds.). (2002). *Between culture and biology.* Cambridge: Cambridge University Press.

Kim, U., Yang, K.-S., & Hwang, K.-K. (Eds.). (2006). *Indigenous and cultural psychology: Understanding people in context.* New York: Springer.

Kitayama, S., & Cohen, D. (Eds.). (2007). *Handbook of cultural psychology.* New York: Guildford Press.

Kitayama, S., & Markus, H. R. (1994). Introduction to cultural psychology and emotion research. In S. Kitayama & H. R. Markus (Eds.), *Emotion and culture: Empirical studies of mutual influence* (pp. 1–19). Washington, DC: American Psychological Association.

Klein, R. A., Ratliff, K. A., Vianello, M., Adams, R. B., Bahnik, Š., Bernstein, M. J. ... Nosek, B. A. (2014). Investigating variation in replicability: A "Many Labs" replication project. *Social Psychology, 45,* 142–152.

Klein, R. A., Vianello, M., Hasselman, F., Adams, B. G., Adams, R. B., Aler, S. ... Nosek, B. A. (2018). Many Labs 2: Investigating variation in replicability across samples and settings. *Advances in Methods and Practices in Psychological Science, 1,* 443–490.

Kroeber, A. L., & Kluckhohn, C. (1952). *Culture: A critical review of concepts and definitions.* Vol. 47, no. 1. Cambridge, MA: Peabody Museum.

Kuhn, T. S. (1962). *The structure of scientific revolutions.* Chicago: University of Chicago Press.

Kuper, A., & Marks, J. (2011). Anthropologists unite! *Nature, 470,* 166–168.

Lakatos, I. (1974). Falsification and the methodology of scientific research programmes. In I. Lakatos & A. Musgrave (Eds.), *Criticism and the growth of knowledge* (pp. 91–196). Cambridge: Cambridge University Press.

Laland, K. N., Odling-Smee, J., & Feldman, M. W. (2000). Niche construction, biological evolution, and cultural change. *Behavioral and Brain Sciences, 23,* 131–146.

Laland, K. N., Uller, T., Feldman, M. W. Sterelny, K., Müller, G. B., Moczek, A. ... Odling-Smee J. (2015). The extended evolutionary synthesis: Its structure, assumptions and predictions. *Proceedings of the Royal Society B: Biological Sciences, 282* (1813): 2015.1019.

Lamb, M. E., & Lewis, C. (2011). The role of parent-child relationships in child development. In M. E. Lamb & M. H. Bornstein (Eds.), *Social and personality development: An advanced textbook* (6th ed., pp. 469–518). New York: Psychology Press.

Lee, J. J., Wedow, R., Okbay, A., Kong, E. M., Maghzian, O., Zacher, M. ... Cesarini-Show, D. (2018). Gene discovery and polygenic prediction from a genome wide association study of educational attainment in 1.1 million individuals. *Nature Genetics, 50,* 1112–1121.

Lerner, R. M., Lewin-Bizan, S., & Warren, A. E. A. (2011). Concepts and theories of human development. In M. H. Bornstein & M. H. Lamb (Eds.). (2011). *Cognitive development: An advanced textbook* (pp. 19–65). New York: Psychology Press.

Leung, K., & Bond, M. H. (2004). Social axioms: A model for social beliefs in multicultural perspective. In M. P. Zanna (Ed.), *Advances in experimental social psychology* (Vol. 36, pp. 119–197). San Diego, CA: Academic Press.

Levinson, S. C. (2003). *Space in language and cognition.* Cambridge: Cambridge University Press.

Lewis, O. (1966). *La vida.* New York: Random House.

Liebal, K., & Haun, D. B. M. (2018). Why cross-cultural psychology is incomplete without comparative and developmental perspectives. *Journal of Cross-Cultural Psychology, 49*, 751–763.

Lindsey, D. T., & Brown, A. M. (2009). World Color Survey color naming reveals universal motifs and their within-language diversity. *PNAS, 106*, 47, 19785–19790.

Lucas, R., & Diener, E. (2008). Can we learn about national differences in happiness from individual responses? A multilevel approach. In F. J. R. Van de Vijver, D. A. Van Hemert, & Y. H. Poortinga (Eds.), *Individuals and cultures in multilevel analysis* (pp. 223–248). Mahwah, NJ: Erlbaum.

Lumsden, C. J., & Wilson, E. O. (1981). *Genes, mind and culture: The coevolutionary process.* Cambridge, MA: Harvard University Press.

Luria, A. K. (1971). Towards the problem of the historical nature of psychological processes. *International Journal of Psychology, 6*, 259–272.

Lutz, C. A. (1988). *Unnatural emotions: Everyday sentiments on a Micronesian atoll and their challenge to Western theory.* Chicago: University of Chicago Press.

Lykken, D. T. (1968). Statistical significance in psychological research. *Psychological Bulletin, 70*(3), 151-159.

Lyman, R. L. (2006). Cultural traits and cultural integration. *Behavioral and Brain Sciences, 29*, 357–358.

Majid, A., Bowerman, M., Kita, S., Haun, D. B. M., & Levinson, S. C. (2004). Can language restructure cognition? The case for space. *Trends in Cognitive Sciences, 8*, 108–114.

Malpass, R. S., & Poortinga, Y. H. (1986). Strategies for design and analysis. In W. J. Lonner & J. W. Berry (Eds.), *Field methods in cross-cultural research* (pp. 47–84). Beverly Hills, CA: Sage.

Manning, A., & Dawkins, M. S. (2012). *An introduction to animal behavior.* Cambridge: Cambridge University Press.

Markus, H. R., & Kitayama, S. (1991). Culture and the self: Implications for cognition, emotion, and motivation. *Psychological Review, 98,* 244–253.

Maseland, R., & Van Hoorn, A. (2009). Explaining the negative correlation between values and practices: A note on the Hofstede-GLOBE debate. *Journal of International Business Studies, 40,* 527–532.

Masuda, T., & Nisbett, R. E. (2001). Attending holistically versus analytically: Comparing the context sensitivity of Japanese and Americans. *Journal of Personality and Social Psychology, 81,* 922–934.

Matsumoto, D. (1999). Culture and self: An empirical assessment of Markus and Kitayama's theory of independent and interdependent self-construals. *Asian Journal of Social Psychology, 2,* 289–310.

Matsumoto, D., & Willingham, B. (2006). The thrill of victory and the agony of defeat: Spontaneous expressions of medal winners at the 2004 Athens Olympic Games. *Journal of Personality and Social Psychology, 91,* 568–581.

Maynard Smith, J., & Harper, D. (2003). *Animal signals.* Oxford: Oxford University Press.

Mayr, E. (1961). Cause and effect in biology. *Science, 134,* 1501–1506.

McCrae, R. R., & Terracciano, A. (2008). The five-factor model and its correlates in individuals and cultures. In F. J. R. Van de Vijver, D. A. Van Hemert, & Y. H. Poortinga (Eds.), *Multilevel analyses of individuals and cultures* (pp. 249–283). Mahwah, NJ: Erlbaum.

McCrae, R. R., Terracciano, A., & 79 Members of the Personality Profiles of Cultures Project. (2005). Personality profiles of cultures: Aggregate personality traits. *Journal of Personality and Social Psychology, 89,* 407–425.

McWhorter, J. H. (2014). *The language hoax.* Oxford: Oxford University Press.

Mesman, J., Minter, T., Angnged, A., Cissé, I. A. H., Salali, G. D., & Migliano, A. B. (2018). Universality without uniformity: A culturally inclusive approach to sensitive responsiveness in infant caregiving. *Child Development, 89,* 837–850.

Mesoudi, A., Whiten, A., & Laland, K. N. (2006). Towards a unified science of cultural evolution. *Behavioral and Brain Sciences, 29,* 329–383.

Milanovic, B. (2009). *Global inequality and the global inequality extraction ratio.* New York: World Bank.

Milfont, T. L., & Klein, R. A. (2018). Replication and reproducibility in cross-cultural psychology. *Journal of Cross-Cultural Psychology, 49,* 735–750.

Miyamoto, Y., & Kitayama, S. (2002). Cultural variation in correspondence bias: The critical role of attitude diagnosticity of socially constrained behavior. *Journal of Personality and Social Psychology, 83,* 1239–1248.

Mkhize, N. (2004). Psychology: An African perspective. In K. Ratele, N. Duncan, D. Hook, N. Mkhize, P. Kiguwa, & A. Collins (Eds.), *Self, community and psychology* (pp. 1–29). Cape Town: UCT Press.

Morris, M. W., Chiu, C-Y. , & Liu, Z. (2015). Polycultural psychology. *Annual Review of Psychology, 66*, 631–659.

Moscovici, S. (1984). The phenomenon of social representations. In R. M. Farr & S. Moscovici (Eds.), *Social representations* (pp. 3–70). Cambridge: Cambridge University Press.

Murata, A., Moser, J., & Kitayama, S. (2013). Culture shapes electrocortical responses during emotion suppression. *Social Cognitive and Affective Neuroscience, 8*, 595–601.

Na, J., Grossmann, I., Varnum, M. E. W., Karasawa, M., Cho, Y., Kitayama, S., & Nisbett, R. E. (2020). Culture and personality revisited: Behavioral profiles and within-person stability in interdependent (vs. independent) social orientation and holistic (vs. analytic) cognitive style. *Journal of Personality, 88*, 908–924.

Na, J., Grossmann, I., Varnum, M. E. W., Kitayama, S., Gonzalez, R., & Nisbett, R. E. (2010). Cultural differences are not always reducible to individual differences. *PNAS 107*(14), 6192–6197.

Nel, J. A., Valchev, V. H., Rothmann, S., van de Vijver, F. J. R., Meiring, D., & de Bruin, G. P. (2012). Exploring the personality structure in the 11 languages of South Africa. *Journal of Personality, 80*(4), 915-948.

Nisbett, R. E. (2003). *The geography of thought: How Asians and Westerners think differently . . . and why.* New York: The Free Press.

Nisbett, R. E., Peng, K. P., Choi, I., & Norenzayan, A. (2001). Culture and systems of thought: Holistic versus analytic cognition. *Psychological Review, 108*, 291–310.

Norenzayan, A., Shariff, A. F., Gervais, W. M., Wilard, A. K., McNamara, R. A., Slingerland, E., & Henrich, J. (2014). The cultural evolution of prosocial religions. *Behavioral and Brain Sciences, 39*, ArtID: e1.

Norenzayan, A., Smith, E. E., Kim, B. J., & Nisbett, R. E. (2002). Cultural preferences for formal versus intuitive reasoning. *Cognitive Science, 26*, 653–684.

Nosek, B. A., Ebersole, C. R., DeHaven, A. C., & Mellor, D. T. (2018). The preregistration revolution. *PNAS, 115*, 2600–2606.

Nowak, M. A. (2006). Five rules for the evolution of cooperation. *Science, 314* (5805), 1560–1563.

Open Science Collaboration. (2015). Estimating the reproducibility of psychological science. *Science 349*, aac4716.

Oxfam. (2015). *Wealth: Having it all and wanting more*. Oxford: Oxfam.

Oyserman, D., Coon, H. M., & Kemmelmeier, M. (2002). Rethinking individualism and collectivism: Evaluation of theoretical assumptions and meta-analyses. *Psychological Bulletin, 128*, 3–72.

Oyserman, D., & Lee, S. W. S. (2008). Does culture influence what and how we think? Effects of priming. *Psychological Bulletin, 134*, 311–342.

Panizza, F. (Ed.). (2005). *Populism and the mirror of democracy*. London: Verso.

Peng, K., & Nisbett, R. E. (1999). Culture, dialectics, and reasoning about contradiction. *American Psychologist, 54*, 741–754.

Penn, D. C., Holyoak, K. J., & Povinelli, D. J. (2008). Darwin's mistake: Explaining the discontinuity between human and nonhuman minds. *Behavioral and Brain Sciences, 31*, 109–178.

Pettigrew, T. F. (2015). In pursuit of three theories: Authoritarianism, relative deprivation, and intergroup contact. *Annual Review of Psychology, 67*, 1–21.

Pettigrew, T. F., & Tropp, L. R. (2006). A meta-analytic test of intergroup contact theory. *Journal of Personality and Social Psychology, 90*, 1–33.

Pew Research Center (2017). What It Takes to Truly Be "One of Us." Available from http://assets.pewresearch.org/wp-content/uploads/sites/2/2017/04/14094140/Pew-Research-Center-National-Identity-Report-FINAL-February-1-2017.pdf. Accessed April 14, 2018.

Piaget, J. (1970). Piaget's theory. In P. H. Mussen (Ed.), *Carmichael's manual of child psychology* (3rd ed., pp. 703–732). New York: Wiley.

Pick, S., & Sirkin, J. (2010). *Breaking the cycle of poverty: The human basis for sustainable development*. New York: Oxford University Press.

Piketty, T. (2014). *Capital in the twenty-first century*. Cambridge, MA: Belknap Press.

Pondicherry Manifesto of Indian Psychology. (2002). www.infinityfoundation.com/mandala/i_es/i_es_corne_manifesto_frameset.htm

Poortinga, Y. H. (1999). Do differences in behavior imply a need for different psychologies? *Applied Psychology, An International Review, 48*, 419–432.

Poortinga, Y. H. (2003). Coherence of culture and generalizability of data: Two questionable assumptions in cross-cultural psychology. In J. Berman & J. Berman (Eds.), *Cross-cultural differences in perspectives on the self*. Vol. 49 of the Nebraska Symposium on Motivation (pp. 257–305). Lincoln: University of Nebraska Press.

Poortinga, Y. H. (2015). Is "culture" a workable concept for (cross-)cultural psychology? *Online Readings in Psychology and Culture, 2*(1).

Poortinga, Y. H., & Soudijn, K. (2002). Behavior-culture relationships and ontogenetic development. In H. Keller, Y. H. Poortinga, & A. Schölmerich (Eds.), *Biology, culture and development: Integrating diverse perspectives* (pp. 320–340). Cambridge: Cambridge University Press.

Poortinga, Y. H., & Van Hemert, D. A. (2001). Personality and culture: Demarcating between the common and the unique. *Journal of Personality, 69*, 1033–1060.

Popper, K. R. (1959). *The logic of scientific discovery.* New York: Basic Books.

Ray, V. F. (1952). Techniques and problems in the study of human color perception. *South Western Journal of Anthropology, 8*, 251–259.

Rayner, K., Li, X. S., Williams, C. C., Cave, K. R., & Well, A. D. (2007). Eye movements during information processing tasks: Individual differences and cultural effects. *Vision Research, 47*, 2714–2726.

Reichenbach, H. (1938). *Experience and prediction.* Chicago: University of Chicago Press.

Rentfrow, P. J., & Jokela, M. (2016). Geographical psychology: The spatial organization of psychological phenomena. *Current Directions in Psychological Science, 25*, 393–398.

Richerson, P. J., & Boyd, R. (2005). *Not by genes alone: How culture transformed evolution.* Chicago: University of Chicago Press.

Rivers, W. H. R. (1901). Vision. In *Physiology and psychology, Part I. Reports of the Cambridge Anthropological Expedition to Torres Straits* (Vol. II). Cambridge: Cambridge University Press.

Roberson, D., Davidoff, J., Davies, I. R. L., & Shapiro, L. R. (2004). The development of color categories in two languages: A longitudinal study. *Journal of Experimental Psychology: General, 133*, 554–571.

Roberson, D., Davies, I., & Davidoff, J. (2000). Color categories are not universal: Replications and new evidence from a stone-age culture. *Journal of Experimental Psychology: General, 129*, 369–398.

Rogoff, D. (2014). Learning by observing and pitching in to family and community endeavors: An orientation. *Human Development, 57*, 150–161.

Rosa, A., & Valsiner, J. (Eds.). (2018). *The Cambridge handbook of sociocultural psychology* (2nd ed.). Cambridge: Cambridge University Press.

Russell, J. A. (1991). Culture and the categorization of emotions. *Psychological Bulletin, 110*, 426–450.

Russell, J. A. (1994). Is there universal recognition of emotion from facial expression? A review of cross-cultural studies. *Psychological Bulletin, 115*, 102–141.

Sahlins, M. (1977). *The use and abuse of biology*. London: Tavistock Publications.

Schimmack, U., Oishi, S., & Diener, E. (2005). Individualism: A valid and important dimension of cultural differences between nations. *Personality and Social Psychology Bulletin, 9,* 17–31.

Schönpflug, U. (Ed.). (2009). *Cultural transmission: Developmental, psychological, social and methodological perspectives*. Cambridge: Cambridge University Press.

Schwandt, T. A., Lincoln, Y. S., & Guba, E. G. (2007). Judging interpretations: But is it rigorous? Trustworthiness and authenticity in naturalistic evaluation. *New Directions for Evaluation, 114,* 11–25.

Schwartz, S. H. (1992). Universals in the content and structure of values: Theoretical advances and empirical tests in 20 countries. In M. P. Zanna (Ed.), *Advances in experimental social psychology* (Vol. 25, pp. 1–65). San Diego, CA: Academic Press.

Schwartz S. H. (2012, Dec.). An overview of the Schwartz theory of basic values. *Online Readings in Psychology and Culture*. https://scholarworks .gvsu.edu/orpc/

Scribner, S. (1979). Modes of thinking and ways of speaking: Culture and logic reconsidered. In R. O. Freedle (Ed.), *New directions in discourse processing* (pp. 223–243). Norwood, NJ: Ablex.

Scribner, S., & Cole, M. (1981). *The psychology of literacy*. Cambridge, MA: Harvard University Press.

Segall, M. H. (1996). Individualism and collectivism: Descriptions or explanations? [Review of the book *Individualism and collectivism*]. *Contemporary Psychology, 41,* 540–542.

Segall, M. H., Campbell, D. T., & Herskovits, K. J. (1966). *The influence of culture on visual perception*. Indianapolis, IN: Bobbs-Merrill.

Segall, M. H., Dasen, P. R., Berry, J. W., & Poortinga, Y. H. (1990). *Human behavior in global perspective: An introduction to cross-cultural psychology*. New York: Pergamon.

Selig, J. P., Card, N. A., & Little, T. D. (2008). Latent structural equation modeling in cross-cultural research: Multigroup and multilevel approaches. In F. J. R. van de Vijver, D. A. van Hemert, & Y. H. Poortinga (Eds.), *Individuals and cultures in multilevel analysis* (pp. 93–119). Mahwah, NJ: Erlbaum.

Sen, A. (1999). *Development as freedom*. New York: Anchor Books.

Shadish, W. R., Cook, T. D., & Campbell, D. T. (2002). *Experimental and quasi-experimental designs for generalized causal inference*. Boston: Houghton Mifflin.

Shweder, R. A. (1984). Preview. In R. A. Shweder & R. A. LeVine (Eds.), *Culture theory: Essays on mind, self, and emotion* (pp. 1–24). Cambridge: Cambridge University Press.

Shweder, R. A. (1990). Cultural psychology – What is it? In J. W. Stigler, R. A. Shweder, & G. Herdt (Eds.), *Cultural psychology: Essays on comparative human development* (pp. 1–43). Cambridge: Cambridge University Press.

Simmons, J. P., Nelson, L. D., & Simonsohn, U. (2011). False-positive psychology: Undisclosed flexibility in data collection and analysis allows presenting anything as significant. *Psychological Science, 22,* 1359–1366.

Simons, R. C., & Hughes, C. C. (1985). Culture bound syndromes. In A. C. Gaw (Ed.), *Culture, ethnicity and mental illness* (pp. 75–93). Washington, DC: American Psychiatric Association Press.

Singh, S., & Tripathi, R. C. (2010). Why do the bonded fear freedom? Some lessons from the field. *Psychology and Developing Societies, 22,* 249–297.

Sinha, D. (1997). Indigenizing psychology. In J. W. Berry, Y. H. Poortinga, & J. Pandey (Eds.), *Handbook of cross-cultural psychology* (2nd ed., Vol. 1, pp. 129–169). Boston: Allyn & Bacon.

Skinner, B. F. (1957). *Verbal behavior.* New York: Appleton-Century-Crofts.

Small, M. L., Harding, D. J., & Lamont M. (2010). Reconsidering culture and poverty. *Annals of the American Academy of Political and Social Science, 629,* 6–27.

Song, R., Moon, S., Chen, H., & Houston, M. B. (2018). When marketing strategy meets culture: The role of culture in product evaluations. *Journal of the Academy of Marketing Science, 46,* 384–402.

Sosis, R., & Bressler, E. (2003). Cooperation and commune longevity: A test of the costly signaling theory of religion. *Cross-Cultural Research, 37,* 211–239.

Soudijn, K. A., Hutschemaekers, G. J. M., & Van de Vijver, F. J. R. (1990). Culture conceptualisations. In F. J. R. Van de Vijver & G. J. M. Hutschemaekers (Eds.), *The investigation of culture: Current issues in cultural psychology* (pp. 19–39). Tilburg, the Netherlands: Tilburg University Press.

Spector, P. E., Cooper, C. L., & Sparks, K. (2001). An international study of the psychometric properties of the Hofstede values survey module 1994. *Applied Psychology: An International Review, 50,* 269–281.

Steenkamp, J.-B. E. M., & Ter Hofstede, F. (2002). International market segmentation: Issues and perspectives. *International Journal of Research in Marketing 19,* 185–213.

Super, C. M. (1976). Environmental effects on motor development: The case of "African infant precocity." *Developmental Medicine and Child Neurology, 18*, 561–567.

Super, C. M., & Harkness, S. (1986). The developmental niche: A conceptualization at the interface of child and culture. *International Journal of Behavioral Development, 9*, 545–569.

Tajfel, H., & Turner, J. C. (1979). An integrative theory of intergroup conflict. In W. G. Austin & S. Worchel (Eds.), *The social psychology of intergroup relations* (pp. 33–47). Monterey, CA: Brooks/Cole.

Takano, Y., & Sogon, S. (2008). Are Japanese more collectivistic than Americans? Examining conformity in in-groups and the reference-group effect. *Journal of Cross-Cultural Psychology, 39*, 237–250.

The Illusions Index. See www.illusionsindex.org/ir/vertical-horizontal-illusion (consulted August 2020).

Tinbergen, N. (1963). On aims and methods of ethology. *Zeitschrift fuer Tierpsychologie, 20*, 410–433.

Tooby, J., & Cosmides, L. (1990). The past explains the present: Emotional adaptations and the structure of ancestral environments. *Ethology and Sociobiology, 11*, 375–424.

Triandis, H. C. (1989). The self and social behavior in differing cultural contexts. *Psychological Review, 96*, 506–520.

Triandis, H. C. (1996). The psychological measurement of cultural syndromes. *American Psychologist, 51*, 407–415.

Trivers, R. L. (1971). The evolution of reciprocal altruism. *Quarterly Review of Biology, 46*, 35–57.

Tsai, J. L., & Clobert, M. (2019). Cultural influences on emotion: Established patterns and emerging trends. In D. Cohen & S. Kitayama (Eds.), *Handbook of cultural psychology* (2nd ed., pp. 292–318). New York: Guildford Press.

Tylor, E. B. (1958). *Primitive culture*. New York: Harper (first published 1871).

United Nations. (2017). *Resolution adopted by the General Assembly on 6 July 2017.*

Valchev, V. H., Van de Vijver, F. J. R., Meiring, D., Nel, J. A., Hill, C., Laher, S. & Adams, B. G. (2014). Beyond Agreeableness: Social–relational personality concepts from an indigenous and cross-cultural perspective. *Journal of Research in Personality 48*, 17–32.

Valsiner, J. (Ed.). (2012). *The Oxford handbook of culture and psychology*. Oxford: Oxford University Press.

Van de Schoot, R., Kaplan, D., Denissen, J., Asendorpf, J. B. Neyer, F. J., & Van Aken, M. A. G. (2014). A gentle introduction to Bayesian analysis: Applications to developmental research. *Child Development, 85*, 842–860.

Van de Vijver, F. J. R., & Leung, K. (1997). *Methods and data analysis for cross-cultural research*. Thousand Oaks, CA: Sage.

Van de Vijver, F. J. R., & Leung, K. (2021). *Methods and data analysis for cross-cultural research* (2nd ed.). Cambridge: Cambridge University Press.

Van de Vijver, F. J. R., Chasiotis A., & Breugelmans, S. M. (Eds.) (2011). *Fundamental questions in cross-cultural psychology*. Cambridge: Cambridge University Press.

Van de Vijver, F. J. R., & Poortinga, Y. H. (1997). Towards an integrated analysis of bias in cross-cultural assessment. *European Journal of Psychological Assessment, 13*, 21–29.

Van de Vijver F. J. R., & Poortinga Y. H. (2020). Dealing with methodological pitfalls in cross-cultural studies of stress. In T. Ringeisen, P. Genkova, & F. Leong (Eds.), *Handbuch Stress und Kultur*. [Handbook stress and culture]. Wiesbaden: Springer.

Van de Vijver, F. J. R., Avvisati, F., Davidov, E., Eid, M., Fox, J.-P., Le Donné, N. . . . Van de Schoot, R. (2019). *Invariance analyses in large-scale studies. OECD Education Working Paper No. 201*. Paris: OECD.

Van de Vijver, F. J. R., Blommaert, J. M. E., Gkoumasi, G., & Stogianni, M. (2015). On the need to broaden the concept of ethnic identity. *International Journal of Intercultural Relations, 46*, 36–46.

Van de Vijver, F. J. R., Van Hemert, D. A., & Poortinga, Y. H. (Eds.). (2008). *Individuals and cultures in multi-level analysis* (pp. 3–26). Mahwah, NJ: Erlbaum.

Van Hemert, D. A., Van de Vijver, F. J. R., & Poortinga, Y. H. (2002). The Beck Depression Inventory as a measure of subjective well-being: A cross-national study. *Journal of Happiness Studies, 3*, 257–286.

Veenhoven, R. (n.d.). *Average happiness in 162 nations 2010–2018*. www .worlddatabaseofhappiness-archive.eur.nl/hap_nat/findingreports/ RankReport_AverageHappiness.php

Verkuyten, M. (2014). *Identity and cultural diversity: What social psychology can teach us*. London: Routledge/Taylor & Francis.

Vertovec, S. (2007). Super-diversity and its implications. *Ethnic and Racial Studies, 30*, 1024–1054.

Vignoles, V. L. Owe, E., Becker, M., Smith, P. B., Easterbrook, M. J., Brown, R. . . . Bond, M. H. (2016). Beyond the "East–West" dichotomy: Global variation in cultural models of selfhood. *Journal of Experimental Psychology: General, 145*, 966–1000.

Voland, E., Chasiotis, A., & Schievenhövel, W. (Eds.). (2005). *Grandmotherhood*. New Brunswick, NJ: Rutgers University Press.

Vul, E., Harris, C., Winkielman, P., & Pashler, H. (2009). Puzzlingly high correlations in fMRI studies of emotion, personality, and social cognition. *Perspectives on Psychological Science, 4*, 274–290.

Vygotsky, L. S. (1978). *Mind in society: The development of higher psychological processes*. Cambridge, MA: Harvard University Press.

Walter, K. V., Conroy-Beam D., Buss, D. M., Asao, K., Sorokowska, A., Sorokowski, P. . . . Zupančič, M. (2020). Sex differences in mate preferences across 45 countries: A large-scale replication. *Psychological Science, 31*, 408–423.

Ward, C. (2008). Thinking outside the Berry boxes: New perspectives on identity, acculturation and intercultural relations. *International Journal of Intercultural Relations, 32*, 105–114.

Wen, H., & Wang, H. (2013). Confucian cultural psychology and its contextually creative intentionality. *Culture & Psychology, 19*, 184–202.

Whiten, A. (2021). The psychological reach of culture in animals' lives. *Current Directions in Psychological Science, 30*, 211–217.

Whiting, J. W. M. (1994). Environmental constraints on infant care practices. In E. H. Chasdi (Ed.), *Culture and human development* (pp. 107–134). Cambridge: Cambridge University Press.

Whorf, B. L. (1956). *Language, thought and reality*. Cambridge, MA: The MIT Press.

Wicherts, J. M., Veldkamp, C. L. S., Augusteijn, H. E. M., Bakker, M., van Aert, R. C. M., & van Assen, M. A. L. M. (2016). Degrees of freedom in planning, running, analyzing, and reporting psychological studies: A checklist to avoid p-hacking. *Frontiers in Psychology, 7*, ArtID: 1832.

Wilkinson, R. G., & Pickett, K. E. (2017). The enemy between us: The psychological and social costs of inequality. *European Journal of Social Psychology, 47*, 11–24.

Wilson, E. O. (1975). *Sociobiology: The new synthesis*. Cambridge, MA: Harvard University Press.

Wilson, H. F. (2017). On geography and encounter: Bodies, borders, and difference. *Progress in Human Geography, 41*, 451–471.

Wong, B. I., Yin, S., Yang, L., Li, J. & Spaniol, J. (2018). Cultural differences in memory for objects and backgrounds in pictures. *Journal of Cross-Cultural Psychology, 49*, 404–417.

Woodworth, R. S., & Schlosberg, H. (1954). *Experimental psychology* (rev. ed.). New York: Holt.

Worthman, C. M. (2010). The ecology of human development: Evolving models for cultural psychology. *Journal of Cross-Cultural Psychology, 41*, 546–562.

Wundt, W. (1913). *Elemente der Völkerpsychologie* (2nd edn.) [Elements of Völkerpsychologie]. Leipzig: Alfred Kroner Verlag.

Zahavi, A., & Zahavi, A. (1997). *The handicap principle: A missing piece of Darwin's puzzle*. Oxford: Oxford University Press.

Acknowledgments

Two fellowships at the Netherlands Institute for Advanced Study in the Humanities and Social Sciences (NIAS, 1984–1985 and September 2004–February 2005) gave me the opportunity to develop the ideas reflected in this Element. A hospitality arrangement at the Department of Organization Sciences of the Vrije Universiteit in Amsterdam facilitated the writing. Numerous colleagues have helped shape my thinking, first and foremost Fons van de Vijver, my close colleague at Tilburg University for many years. Kenneth Keith, editor of the CUP Elements Series, Ron Fischer, and anonymous reviewers commented on an earlier draft. Linda Benson competently copyedited the manuscript and Aloysias Thomas handled the editing process. I am most grateful for all the support that I received.

Cambridge Elements ☰

Psychology and Culture

Kenneth D. Keith
University of San Diego
Kenneth D. Keith is author or editor of more than 160 publications on cross-cultural psychology, quality of life, intellectual disability, and the teaching of psychology. He was the 2017 president of the Society for the Teaching of Psychology.

About the Series
Elements in Psychology and Culture features authoritative surveys and updates on key topics in cultural, cross-cultural, and indigenous psychology. Authors are internationally recognized scholars whose work is at the forefront of their subdisciplines within the realm of psychology and culture.

Cambridge Elements $^{\equiv}$

Psychology and Culture

A full series listing is available at: www.cambridge.org/EPAC

CPSIA information can be obtained
at www.ICGtesting.com
Printed in the USA
BVHW042036261021
619939BV00006B/50

9 781108 827614